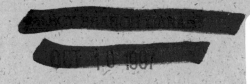

A Sketch of the Life and Character
of Daniel Boone

Also by Ted Franklin Belue

The Long Hunt: Death of the Buffalo East of the Mississippi

A Sketch of the Life and Character of Daniel Boone

by
Peter Houston

Edited by
Ted Franklin Belue

STACKPOLE
BOOKS

Published by
STACKPOLE BOOKS
5067 Ritter Road
Mechanicsburg, PA 17055

Printed in the United States of America

10 9 8 7 6 5 4 3 2 1

FIRST EDITION

Library of Congress Cataloging-in-Publication Data

Houston, Peter, 1761-1855.
 A sketch of the life and character of Daniel Boone / by Peter Houston; edited
by Ted Franklin Belue. — 1st ed.
  p. cm.
 Originally written in 1842 as a letter in response to a request from the author's
grandson.
 Includes bibliographical references and index.
 ISBN 0-8117-1522-1
 1. Boone, Daniel, 1734-1820—Anecdotes. 2. Pioneers—Kentucky—
Biography—Anecdotes. 3. Kentucky—Biography—Anecdotes. 4. Frontier
and pioneer life—Kentucky—Anecdotes. 5. Kentucky—History—Revolution,
1775-1783—Anecdotes. 6. United States—History—Revolution, 1775-1783—
Anecdotes. I. Belue, Ted Franklin. II. Title.
F454.B66H68 1997
976.9'02—dc20   96-42539
                                CIP

To my friend Chance Watson, slain in the flower of his youth while defending his wife and child. May he long be remembered.

Credits

Versions of material used herein in several footnotes appeared previously in Ted Franklin Belue, *The Long Hunt: Death of the Buffalo East of the Mississippi* (Mechanicsburg, PA: Stackpole Books, 1996); and Ted Franklin Belue, "Indian-Influenced Woodsmen of the Cane," *Book of Buckskinning VII* (Texarkana, TX: Scurlock Publishing, 1995).

Contents

Acknowledgments

Many hands other than my own went into the making of this little tome, and those folks must be thanked. Foremost is Mrs. Gladys Santen, of Paris, Kentucky, the great-great-great-granddaughter of Peter Houston. On the hot afternoon of June 21, 1996, Mrs. Santen and her husband, John, although they had little warning of our coming, took my wife and me into their lovely Victorian home and treated us cordially. As I sat on an antique chair, musing, sipping iced tea garnished with mint and lemon, resting my glass on a napkin on top of a marble-topped wood table once owned by F. W. Houston, Mrs. Santen fielded questions about genealogy and local history. Her contributions pushed wide a long-shut door of transcendence, and her beaten biscuits and deviled ham, a perennial Kentucky delight, soothed the gnaw in our stomachs.

Also of Paris, Betty Sosby, curator and hostess of Duncan Tavern, showed me Michael Stoner's old Kentucky rifle (converted from flint-lock to percussion but otherwise intact), Squire Boone's brass snuff box, and other curious relics, including a rare, half-finished buffalo-horn powder horn. Historically minded readers who travel should note that Duncan's Tavern, built in 1788 on a wide buffalo path known then as Clark's War Road for General George Rogers Clark and now as Highway 68, was frequented by the likes of Daniel and Squire Boone, Simon Kenton, Michael Stoner, Peter Houston, and his brothers.

Lucy Cooper, of the Bourbon County Chamber of Commerce, directed my wife and me to the stone obelisk in Paris marking the site of Houston's Station. Erected by the swirling Hopewell spring whose cool, algae-filled waters slip into the nearby cascades of Houston Creek, the twelve-foot pillar, shaded by a stand of mulberry trees, now rises from behind a greasy auto shop and cable television satellite center. The spot is obscurely known by locals as "a place where Indians were."

Thanks too to the four anonymous "'backer" farmers from Sharpsburg who hauled my pickup out of a muddy ditch I had buried it in when, en route to Mrs. Santen's house, I suddenly pulled to the shoulder to save from traffic a snapping turtle trekking westbound across Highway 406. May the rescued snapper and his irascible kind live long and prosper and stay off the asphalt.

Other folks lent a strong hand to my efforts. H. David Wright, artist extraordinaire of Gray Stone Press, in Nashville, Tennessee, gave his time, talents, and energy re-creating for the jacket the only authentic full-length Boone portrait extant, *Col. Daniel Boon.*, originally engraved and painted by Chester Harding and James Otto Lewis in October 1820. Dr. Jerry A. Herndon, Professor of English at Murray State University, in Murray, Kentucky, proofed the draft twice; his patience, tireless efforts, laconic wit, and sharp eyes remain some of my biggest assets. Hal Rice and David E. Smith, also of Murray, helped with photographs and illustrations. Ken Kamper, of Hazelwood, Missouri, historian for the Daniel Boone and Frontier Families Research Association, contributed Boone genealogical data; Ken's insights and efforts are singular, and recognition for him is long overdue. Michael J. Taylor, a peerless Cincinnati artisan of eighteenth-century Woodland Indian crafts, provided knowledge of the old ways. Nancy O'Malley, of the Department of Archaeology, at the University of Kentucky, gave me permission to use her plat of Houston's Station. Dr. Nelson W. Dawson, of the Filson Club in Louisville, Kentucky, granted me use of a map of the Transylvania purchase as rendered by Kentucky historian, architect, and famed white water canoeist, Neal O. Hammon. Jack Turbeville, of Shepherdsville, Kentucky, prepared one map appearing in the text. My wife, Lavina, who is Jack's daughter, put up with me during the days and nights I was buried under reels of microfilmed copies of the Draper Manuscripts ferreting out arcane bits of information about Daniel Boone and Peter Houston. Nor did she flinch when I let loose a blue streak the night I erased both copies of my tediously transcribed transcript of Houston's memoirs from my computer disks and had to start over from scratch.

Introduction

My highly esteemed grandson, your letter of recent date in behalf of William Falls Thornton who seeks for information relating to the life and character of Daniel Boone was duly received and my answer is as follows. . . .[1]

THUS WROTE PETER HOUSTON TO HIS GRANDSON, FRANKLIN WARREN Houston, on May 2, 1842.

Peter Houston was born, according to his grandson's chronology, on April 2, 1761. In the spring of 1769, Daniel Boone, John Findley, John Stewart, and three camp tenders led a string of packhorses through the Cumberland Gap into *Kanta-ke* and into history. The same year that Boone and his men crossed the Blue Ridge for their first Kentucky long hunt, Houston's family—descended from a line of Calvinist emigrants named Houseson who arrived at Jamestown in 1612 from Dublin, Scotland—left the Shenandoah Valley of Virginia. In May 1769, Samuel Houston, with his wife Sarah and their children (ultimately Samuel and Sarah had five sons, including Peter, and three daughters) settled on a farm in Iredell County, North Carolina, just across from the farm belonging to Daniel Boone's father, Squire Boone, Sr., along the Yadkin River in Rowan County.[2]

Daniel, along with his younger brother, Squire, Jr., who had joined the others in Kentucky the fall of 1769 after he harvested the crops, returned in 1771, broke but not broken, their traps, guns, and peltry confiscated by Indians. Daniel farmed, market hunted, trapped, and commercial fished for the next two years, itching for his next stab at Kentucky. Meanwhile, the Boones got to know the Houstons. Young Peter Houston idolized Daniel, who, in turn, grew fond of the boy.

Boone first tried to settle Kentucky in 1773. Five families followed him; others joined along the way as the caravan split up into three groups and wound up and over the Blue Ridge. In the dawn mists of October 10, a band of about twenty Delaware, Shawnee, and Cherokee fired on the rear bunch of Carolinians, killing Boone's sixteen-year-old son, James, John and Richard Mendinall, Henry Russell, and a slave. Boone turned the travelers back, and they settled along the Clinch. "My footsteps have often been marked with blood," he told his first biographer, John Filson, in 1783, recalling the brutal loss of his firstborn.

In 1774, new raids ignited by the slaying of the family of Mingo chieftain John Logan swept across western Virginia to the Holston River. On June 26, Clinch militia leader Captain William Russell dispatched Boone and Michael Stoner to Kentucky to warn the teams of Virginia surveyors who were in the Bluegrass mapping the region of the hostilities that were later known as Lord Dunmore's War. Boone found the men at the fledgling settlement of Harrod's Town, he reported, "well drove in by the Indians." By this time Boone knew the lay of Kentucky better than any other white man.

Then came lawyer Richard Henderson, the Transylvania Land Company, and the illegal Treaty of Sycamore Shoals which violated Crown law, Virginia law, the Treaty of 1763, and the Fort Stanwix Treaty (1768). In March 1775, Cherokee elders—though some of them, most notably Oconostota, recanted and denied their deeds—sold their Kentucky hunting claims for ten thousand pounds worth of silver and trade goods to Henderson and his well-heeled gang of land pirates. By May 1775, Boone, now an employee of Henderson, and aided by his oldest daughter Susannah and a slave woman as camp cooks, led thirty trail-blazing axmen along a maze of buffalo traces cutting from the Holston through the Cumberland Gap and to the Kentucky River and began felling logs to erect Kentucky's first fort—Boonesborough. By the end of 1775, Boone's wife, Rebecca, and their children joined Daniel at the outpost, the cutting edge of America's Far West.

On a Sunday afternoon in July 1776, Shawnee and Cherokee warriors kidnapped Boone's daughter Jemima and two of Colonel Richard Callaway's girls, Fanny and Betsy, from a canoe on the Kentucky. Boone led a force of Kentuckians to rescue the teenage trio before the Indians ferried them across the Ohio. Well known even then as a hunter, scout, and a good hand in an Indian fight, Boone became a hero. Indeed, the rescue of the Boone and Callaway girls was the stuff of which legends are made; author James Fenimore Cooper immortalized a modified version of the tale in 1826 in *The Last of the Mohicans*.

Since then, novelists, artists, and Hollywood have exploited the "savage Indians capturing the helpless white girls" theme many times over.

1777. Remembered by Kentuckians as the bloody Year of the Three Sevens. Twelve deadly months boiling with worry, treachery, and intrigue. Shawnees attacked the cabins and forts of the white trespassers, killed, stole the settlers' horses or took back their own ponies that had been stolen from them, slaughtered livestock, and burned crops. Indians shot Boone during a raid on Boonesborough on April 24. The ball shattered his ankle and Boone collapsed, but Simon Kenton, a strapping, rawboned youth, scooped the stout woodsman up in his arms like a child and lugged him to safety.

On October 6, 1777, American blackguards murdered Cornstalk, chief of the Maquachake Shawnee, his son Elinipsico, and two friends, Red Hawk and Petall, under a flag of truce at Fort Randolph on the Kanawha River in western Virginia. Outraged, Indians took up the hatchet anew. Whites retaliated, sparking ambushes, atrocities, and torchings on both sides of the Ohio. Warriors pledged to avenge Cornstalk's death, drive out the intruders, and take back their Kentucky hunting lands.

Black Fish, the subchief Chalahgawtha (Chillicothe) Shawnee leader who succeeded Cornstalk, plotted vengeance in the form of a winter assault against Kentuckians. He gathered his forces. By early February 1778, he and 120 warriors, a few French partisans, and Pompey, an African ex-slave who lived with the Shawnee as their kinsman and served as interpreter, crossed the Ohio with plans to burn Boonesborough and take the settlers back to Shawnee land. But two days' travel from the fort, Black Fish's scouts spied Boone alone and on foot, leading a horse laden with buffalo beef, and seized him, forcing him to give up his twenty-six men camped at the Lower Blue Licks making salt.

No shots had been fired. No blood was spilled. Black Fish, pleased at his coup, went no further with his plans. The gloating warriors recrossed the icy Ohio, their half-starved white stragglers in tow, and returned in glory to the Shawnee towns.

Black Fish adopted Boone. The Indians marched fourteen of the Kentuckians to Detroit to sell to the British as prisoners of war. They adopted the rest.

Back at the Lower Blue Licks, two couriers, Thomas Brooks and Flanders Callaway, came upon the lonely camp, read the ominous signs, and galloped back to Boonesborough to spread the sad tidings. Settlers forted up, scared, unsure, not knowing the men's fate. By summer two of the hostages escaped back to Kentucky. They told all, casting Boone in a bad light. After enduring gossip and fearing for her husband's safety, Rebecca Boone and her children, except Jemima, packed and fled to the refuge of her father's farm in the Yadkin.

On June 16, Daniel Boone—dressed "Indian-stile," his tawny hair plucked and roached into a scalp lock—dashed away on a horse and pounded "straight as a leather thong" for the flooded Ohio. In four days, Boone the white Shawnee hallooed Boonesborough's stockade and walked in to a crowd of hateful stares and murmurs. The fort was as he had left it in January: timbers rotted, walls in disrepair, no well dug, few loop holes cut, scant precautions taken. Shawnee painted for war were coming, Boone warned the settlers.

But then—a reprieve. Black Fish delayed. Boone snatched the moment to plan defenses, strengthen the fort, dig a well, cut loops in the palisades for sharpshooters, and dispatch riders to Harrod's Town and Logan's Station for men and powder and ball. Kentuckians dug in to wait for Black Fish to make his move.

On September 7, Black Fish, over four hundred warriors, several Frenchmen and British rangers, and Pompey, the black Shawnee, filed over a bluff three hundred yards from Boonesborough. They called for Shel-to-wee, Boone's Shawnee name, which means "Big Turtle." Two days of sham talks slipped by. When Indians grabbed Boone and seven whites parleying in an arbor near the fort, a burst of shots from Boonesborough kindled a nine-day tempest. The Kentuckians held on, day and night dealing blow for blow against frontal assault, hailstorms of lead, showers of fire arrows, torches, incessant sniping, and a nearly successful attempt to tunnel under the fort to blow it up, all the while fighting their own hunger, thirst, fatigue, and terror. But by dawn Friday, September 17, the Indians had given up and slipped away, burying their dead beyond the Kentucky River. All but one—Pompey. William Collins, a noted sharpshooter, drilled the taunting black sniper in the forehead. His native kinsmen left Pompey on the riverbank where Collins dropped him.

Kentuckians suffered two killed in the eleven-day debacle—David Bundrin and London, a valiant slave owned by Richard Henderson—and four wounded: Daniel, Squire, and Jemima Boone, and Pemberton Rollins. But the siege was lifted, and settlers offered up prayers of joyous thanksgiving. Yet, at this juncture of gladness, Boone's days darkened.

Colonel Richard Callaway, whose two nephews remained hostages among the Shawnee, bore Boone no good will. Boone's actions proved that he was in league with the British, Callaway contended, poisoning the tiny community with his accusations. At Logan's Station a month after the siege, militia leaders tried Boone in a court-martial. Boone offered his own defense: He had outwitted Black Fish, saved Boonesborough from attack, and saved his men. Had he not, Boone argued, stood with the fort's defenders during the siege? The jury cleared him of the four charges Callaway had trumped up and promoted him to major of the militia—a resounding vindication of his honor and position.

By November 9, Boone was in North Carolina with his family. He stayed for a year, all the time planning his return to Kentucky. Land, game, adventure, and opportunity beckoned, and one hundred folks seeking a new life joined him. And so it was that in the fall of 1779, when Boone, age forty-five, headed back to Kentucky, Peter Houston, age eighteen, and his two brothers, Robert and James, went with him.

In Kentucky the Houstons fought Indians, hunted, bought land, built a fort, tanned deer and buffalo hides, made salt, eked out a living, married and raised families, and lived out their days west of the Blue Ridge. Peter fought under Boone's command at the Battle of Blue Licks in 1782, hunted with him, and remained his friend until 1799, when the woodsman left Kentucky for Spanish Missouri. Boone died on September 26, 1820, at age eighty-five.

In 1842, while living in Bloomington, Indiana, Peter Houston received an important request from his grandson, Franklin Warren Houston (1818–1903), known as F. W. to family and friends. Attorney William Falls Thornton of Paris, Kentucky, planned to write a book about Daniel Boone and had asked F. W., who lived in North Middletown, Kentucky, to help him gather the reminiscences of Kentuckians who had known the woodsman.

Peter Houston's detailed response to F. W.'s request grew into a personal memoir, but one that kept Boone strongly on center stage, beginning with Boone's Kentucky forays and ending about 1799, when he and his kin left for Missouri. By the time Peter finished his task, his handwritten letter, which he titled "A Sketch of the Life and Character of Daniel Boone," was more than seventy pages long.

When F. W. received the manuscript, he penned a handwritten copy for Thornton and kept the original. In time, F. W. wrote another draft and sent it back to his grandfather. But Thornton's Boone biography was never written; the young attorney died soon after he received Houston's narrative, and his copy of the manuscript disappeared.

In 1855, Peter Houston died. With him vanished his copy of the narrative sent to him by his grandson. Houston's obituary summed up the mettle of this venerable gentleman who left the Presbyterian Church during Kentucky's Great Revival (a regional spinoff of the Great Awakening) in 1801 at Cane Ridge to join with those New Testament disciples there seeking to restore nondenominational Christianity.[3]

> Departed from this life . . . February 1855, Peter Houston, aged 90 years, two months, and 15 days. The deceased was one of the number, who united with Barton W. Stone on the Bible alone, at old Cane Ridge, at the time of the "great revival." And up to the day of his death he lived a very devoted Christian life.[4]

In 1887, historian Dr. Lyman Copeland Draper, perhaps hoping to finish his biography, *Life of Boone*, wrote to F. W. Houston to glean from him a few of his grandfather's memories.[5] F. W. again transcribed his grandfather's memoir and sent the copy to Draper on November 14, 1887. About three weeks later, F. W. decided to take the original manuscript to a Cincinnati bookbinder. Near Paris, a thief snatched from F. W.'s buggy the satchel that held the memoir and other documents. F. W. offered a $10 reward for the return of his property, but to no avail. Fortunately, Draper received his copy, jotted a few notes in the text, and filed this, the only surviving copy of the memoir, away in his collection.

Fragment of a note to Dr. Lyman C. Draper from F. W. Houston regarding Peter Houston's narrative. (DRAPER MANUSCRIPTS, 20C:89{1}, COURTESY THE STATE HISTORICAL SOCIETY OF WISCONSIN)

Lyman Draper never finished his own proposed *Life of Boone*. Nor did he do much with the Houston memoir. Such was typical of Draper, one of America's first oral historians, who wrote just one book out of the dozen or so that he proposed and spent the rest of his days gathering pioneer reminiscences, documents, clippings, signatures, and miscellany for inclusion in his trove of trans-Appalachian Americana.[6] For one hundred years, Peter Houston's "A Sketch of the Life and Character of Daniel Boone" has been tucked away in the Draper Manuscript Collection in the Daniel Boone Papers.

I happened upon the old letter in 1990. Despite its flaws and romantic asides, for a Boone historian and student of the eighteenth century, Houston's "Sketch" was a revelation! Written in F. W.'s bold hand throughout its worn pages are hair-raising tales of wild exploit, new Boone lore, woodsmen's skills, a fresh firsthand look at the devastating Battle of Blue Licks, insights on how settlers tanned hides, precise details regarding dress, religion, lore, language, and other aspects of frontier Kentuckiana.

Excited and intrigued by the discovery, and feeling that Houston's work merited exposure to a broader audience, I began the task of transcribing the memoir, which presented several challenges in interpretation. First, there is Peter's sketchy recall, an issue not overlooked by F. W., who noted to Draper on December 12, 1887:

> The memory, whatever the age, is treacherous, and especially so is the memory of the aged. . . . Whilst my grandfather was noted for great memory and was possessed of a wonderful fund of miscellaneous knowledge, still his memory is not to be cited as an exception to the rule.[7]

At times Peter waxes a bit too eloquent, painting a romantic, strongly heroic Boone tapestry, rich in metaphor, heavy with hyperbole, sure to tug the heartstrings of those who revel in the hunt, the sanctity of hearth and home and of kith and kin.

But it is worth noting that it was only at his grandson's behest that Houston wrote his sketch, which was kept as an heirloom; he did not write his essay to sell. He talks little about himself, focusing mostly on Boone. His anecdotes can be corroborated and accepted or disproved and discarded, according to more reliable sources. Rightly discerned, then, Houston's memoir becomes a rare glimpse of Boone and, even more so, of frontier life.

Besides Peter Houston's age, other literary influences may have clouded his remembrances. When he wrote his Boone sketch, Filson's *Kentucke* was available, and John Trumball's popular, heavily edited version of Filson's "Boon" had gone through at least a dozen editions. In 1822, Lord Byron's *Don Juan* had extolled the virtues of "The General Boon, back-woodsman of Kentucky." John A. McClung featured Boone in 1832 in his *Sketches of Western Adventure*. In 1833, Timothy Flint's *Biographical Memoir of Daniel Boone* was released. How much these works colored Houston's memoirs cannot be known; he must have been aware of at least some of them.

New problems occurred when F. W. Houston rewrote his grandfather's narrative. As he noted to Dr. Draper on November 2, 1887, the old manuscript had "been written in bad ink . . . and subjected to the ravages of forty five years." Some words, dates, and sentences were illegible. Not wanting to send the original, F. W. secured a volume of *Daniel Boone: Pioneer of Kentucky*, by John S. C. Abbott (published in 1872 by a New York press), and used this book as a guide to fill in dates and words in a few places as he penned a new copy, thus repeating Abbott's errors.[8] For example, in Abbott's account of the Battle of Blue Licks (August 19, 1782), two of Boone's sons, Israel and Samuel, were shot; Samuel lived but Israel died. In truth, Samuel Boone, who escaped, was Boone's nephew. In F. W.'s version of the Blue Licks debacle, he inserted Abbott's mistake. Similarly, when Edward "Ned" Boone was shot and decapitated by Indians in October 1780, Abbott wrongly asserted that it was Daniel's youngest brother, Squire, and F. W. repeated Abbott's mistake. To avoid creating any new Boone myths or errors, I used Abbott's *Boone* to pinpoint such flaws in the narrative. I corrected any textual errors and footnoted the revisions.[9]

My goal in editing the memoir was twofold: to preserve its lively flow and to make the text accurate. Except for rare exceptions, spelling, punctuation, and paragraphing remain intact. Wrong names and dates I have unobtrusively corrected and footnoted, but without inserting brackets in the text or the boldly intrusive [*sic*]; to put in visual speed bumps by bracketing every jot and tittle would shatter the homespun integrity of Houston's memoir. Nor did I make any attempt to "improve" Houston's literary style or in any other way alter the narrative voice of one who speaks so strongly and expresses himself so well. Where it was impossible to identify a word in the microfilm copy of the manuscript, I used ellipses.

Annotated end notes abound to correct, clarify, and amplify names, places, persons, and events. Dr. Draper's few notes also appear in the end notes. These I have left intact with the exception of abbreviations, which I have spelled out.

An appendix features the previously unpublished letters of Peter and F. W. Houston and of Draper, as well as Theodore O'Hara's poem "The Old Pioneer, Daniel Boone," which F. W. also mailed to Dr. Draper. Scrutiny of such miscellany helps place Houston's memoir in its larger historical context and will allow readers to see its evolution as it changed hands. And too, curious tidbits contained in the correspondence reveal much about the life and character of Peter Houston, which is important to establish his veracity. A list of selected works about Boone, Kentucky frontier life, and the Anglo settlement of trans-Appalachia appears in the back of the book.

So it was, then, in November 1778, that Boone had returned from Boonesborough to the Yadkin Valley of North Carolina. One year later he led one hundred men, women, and children beyond the Blue Ridge and to the Bluegrass. With him was his wife, Rebecca, and their children, many families of North Carolinians, and three of the Houston boys: Robert the older, James the younger, and Peter the middle-born.

Houston's Narrative:

"A Sketch of the Life and Character of Daniel Boone"

SQUIRE BOONE—FATHER OF DANIEL—AND HIS FAMILY LEFT Pennsylvania in 1750 and located in what is now called Yadkin County, North Carolina.[1] My father, Samuel Houston—his wife and one child (Prudence)—left Shenandoah, Virginia, and located in what is now called Iredell County, North Carolina, on May 9, 1769. The two families soon became intimate as they lived within a few miles of each other, as the early settlers became intimate.

Daniel Boone was married to Rebecca Bryan on August 14, 1756—nine years before I was born.[2] After he married he built a cabin one mile from his father's, cleared a spot of land and raised a little corn and a few vegetables and hunted much for a livelihood until John Findley, who with a small party—had traversed a part of Kentucky—returned to our community and gave a glowing account of the country and the wild game he had seen.[3] His description enthused Daniel Boone who never rested until he formed a party and set out to explore the enchanting land for himself. His party consisted of John Findley, William Coolie, Joseph Holder, John Muncey, John Stewart and himself.[4] And on May 1, 1769, they bade adieu to families and friends, Boone leaving his wife and five children at his father's. Whilst exploring Kentucky Boone and Stewart having left their camp alone were captured by Indians and held for some days. But they escaped, and when they returned they found their comrades were gone and their camp plundered. Their comrades were never heard of afterwards.[5]

The following year Squire Boone—Daniel's brother—and William Sconce left our neighborhood and joined Daniel and Stewart—the remnant of the party—in Kentucky; and in a skirmish with the Indians shortly afterwards between Boone and Stewart and Indians, Stewart was killed. This frightened Sconce and he started for home, but he was never heard of afterward.[6] This left but two of the eight adventurers, Daniel Boone and his brother Squire. Their ammunition gave out and Squire went home to his family and returned with a fresh supply and a horse. They continued to explore until they became so enraptured by their discoveries that they determined to return home and move their families to Kentucky.

Accordingly, in May 1771, they reached their families.[7]

It was not, however, until the 25th day of September 1773 that they got in readiness for starting.[8] On that day, early in the morning Daniel and wife and six children, Squire Boone and his wife and three children, and several other families, together with 40 men—hunters from Powell's Valley—66 in all—left old Squire Boone's, accompanied, half the day by several of the neighbors; among them Daniel's mother.[9] And when a halt was called for a separation they threw their arms around each other's neck and tears flowed freely from all eyes. Even Daniel, in spite of his brave and manly heart was seen to lift the lapel of his pouch to dry the tears from his eyes whilst his dear old mother held around his neck weeping bitterly. Daniel was devoted to her and she loved Daniel above all her children.

Boone ordered his men to fire a salute and they moved forward whilst the neighbors returned in sadness to their homes.

I need not recite the disaster that befell the immigrants two weeks afterwards—on the 10th of October—near the Cumberland Gap. Boone has told the story and the historian has repeated it. Seven young men and boys were in the rear driving 26 cattle, they halted to gather grapes and black haws. The Indians fell upon them and killed and scalped six and wounded the seventh one. The discharge of the Indians guns brought the advance back but too late to rescue the unfortunate victims except the wounded boy who met them by the way.[10] James Boone, oldest son of Daniel and my cousin James L. Brown were among the killed.[11]

The women and most of the men were so terrified by the horrible scene that Boone was constrained to return to the valley of Clinch River where he remained with his family until the following spring when all returned to the homes they had left.[12]

Boone made no further attempt to move to Kentucky until the spring of 1775.[13] Meantime, in 1774 he and Michael Stoner were appointed by Governor Dunmore of Virginia to go to the Falls and rescue from danger a body of forty surveyors whom he had sent there to survey and parcel out land to immigrants 400 acres having been offered to each immigrant who would settle in Kentucky and pay 40 pounds

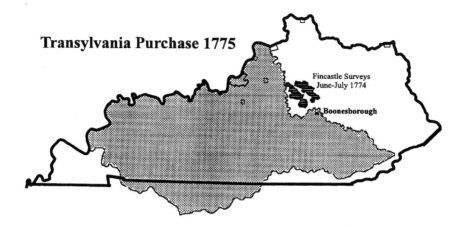

sterling per 100 acres.[14] They started on June 27, 1774, and returned the last week of August following, having lost but one man by the Indians.[15]

Boone was next employed by Richard Henderson, who was at the head of what was called "the Transylvania Land Company" to meet the Indian chiefs, who claimed all the land between the Kentucky and Cumberland Rivers, and purchase from them, in the name of the company.[16] This with . . . of country, agreeing to give Boone for his services a certain boundary of land near Boonesborough.[17] Accordingly in March of 1775 Boone met the Indians at Watauga and on March 17 the treaty was signed.[18]

He was then employed by the company to open a road from the Holston Valley in Tennessee to Boonesborough to facilitate immigration. He employed help and soon accomplished this work.[19] He then enlarged and fortified Boonesborough and returned to his family on the

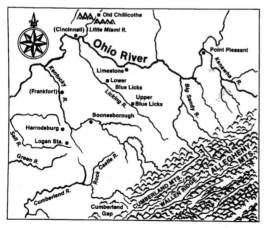

Yadkin with the view of reserving his effort to move them to Boonesborough, and the 23rd day of September 1775 he with his wife and seven children—the youngest an infant—in company with several other families started on his journey and on October 20 arrived safely at the fort.[20]

From this time on until February 1778 I must refer you to the historian for an account of Boone's work in fighting Indians and aiding immigrants as no other man in Kentucky did or could do.[21]

On the 7th of February 1778, he and 28 companions were captured by the Indians whilst making salt at the Blue Licks and taken to Chillicothe, Ohio, and there held as prisoners until he learned that they were plotting an assault on Boonesborough. He then determined to escape and reach the fort in time to prepare to meet the savages. And when he went out the next morning to take his usual hunt, which he for sometime had been permitted to do, he made all possible haste to the Ohio River, found an old canoe, patched it up with mud, crossed the river and reached the fort in safety on the 11th of June 1778, summoned all the available help from other stations, put the fort in a good state of defense and awaited the Indians.[22] They not appearing he, in a few days, went with a small party on a reconnoitering expedition and having reached the Scioto River in Ohio he met, what he regarded as the advance guard of the Indians, put them to flight, and with all possible dispatch returned to the fort.[23]   And on September 7 the Indians arrived, near 500 strong commanded by General Duquesne who immediately demanded from Boone a surrender of the fort.[24] Boone declined, and a messenger then informed Boone that Duquesne had been ordered by General Hamilton [the] British commander—to take the fort, treat with its inmates and do them no harm—and that if Boone with eight of his principal men would come out and enter into a treaty he would then withdraw his forces.[25] Boone feared the proposal was treacherous; but concluded to risk it rather than undertake to defend the fort with fifty-two men against near 500 and agreed to accept the terms.[26] Accordingly Boone and his companions unarmed, marched out, but not until he had posted "sharp shooters" to fire on the Indians should they attempt violence. But as soon as Boone and party clasped hands with an equal number of the savages (which was the Indians' seal to a treaty) they endeavored to drag them to the Indians in the rear. Immediately a volley from the fort brought down four of the treacherous savages, and in the confusion that followed Boone and his men escaped into the fort all unhurt except Daniel's brother Squire who was shot just as he entered the fort.[27] Then began a siege which lasted nine days during which time two of Boone's men were killed and four wounded and 35 of the enemy were killed and a great many wounded. Despairing of success, the Indians raised the siege on September 18, and left the state, and this was the last assault on Boonesborough.[28]

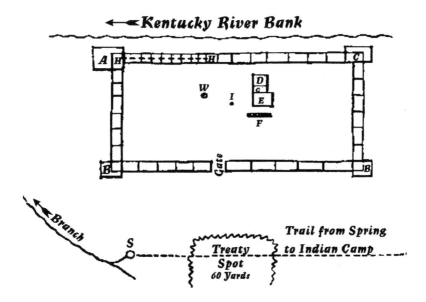

A-Henderson's Kitchen; B.-Two-Story Bastion; C.-Phelp's House;
D.-Squire Boone's House; E.-Colonel Callaway's House; F.-Ball Battery;
G.-Boone's Gun Shop; H.-Ditch or Countermine; I.-Flagstaff;
W.-Well; S.-Sulphur Spring

Moses Boone's Sketch of Fort Boonesborough, c. 1778 (Moses Boone map copied by Neal O. Hammon)

Having achieved this remarkable victory and believing the fort safe against Indian warfare, Boone at once determined to follow his wife and family to the Yadkin and return with them to Boonesborough (where [referring to the Yadkin] they had gone during his captivity, believing he had been put to death by the Indians) and by November 9, 1778, he met his disconsolate wife and children at her father's.[29]

In a few days he sold his four hundred and fifty acres of wild land to a land buyer from Virginia for which he received several thousand dollars in what was called "war scrip" but so depreciated was it in value that the whole amount equaled only $1,000.00 of gold. With this he determined to secure a title to the tract of land given him by Henderson for his services (it having turned out that the Governor of Virginia had pronounced the purchase by Boone for Henderson was "null and void" except as to the Indians) and having no title to the land on which he had squatted Boone therefore was compelled to repurchase from the State or lose his land, and on the 14th day of December he started for Richmond to secure his title, and to . . . for some others who had entrusted him with their money. But at an inn in Charlotte County where he lodged on the night of the 19th he was robbed of all the money he possessed. There were five other guests at the inn—kept by John Jacoby—one a footman, the others had come on horse-back. Boone being fatigued he asked permission to lie on his buffalo rug before the fire and there slept until morning. He ate his breakfast as did all the five who had come on horseback. The footman had left before the family awoke. After breakfast Boone felt for his small change and it was gone out of his pocket. He then felt for his roll of money in another pocket and that was gone. The alarm was raised and all assisted him for four days in hunting for the man who was afoot; all believing that he was the thief, but no trace was ever found of him.[30]

Boone returned to his family completely unmoved—more from the fact that others than himself were to suffer.

Being now destitute of means and having no valid title to his Henderson land he removed to the Yadkin until the fall of 1779 when he determined to move his family to Kentucky and commence life again.[31] He therefore made arrangements to start on September 22 and my older brother Robert and my younger brother James and myself were to go with him. Brother Robert and I had been with our father for two years in a commissary department in the Revolutionary War, and our father having determined to move to Kentucky as soon as the war ended (a purpose, however he never carried out) and not being at liberty to leave his post at this time he sent us home with a letter of instruction to Boone to take his three oldest sons with him to Kentucky and locate them and have them to build a cabin and clear a spot of ground ready to fetch a crop of corn in the spring. We were at Squire Boone's, therefore on the 22nd—ready and eager for the journey. And besides us and Daniel, his wife, and nine children, there were Levy Dickey and wife, John Dobson's wife and two children.[32] John Longnecker, William Bryan and wife (brother-in-law to Boone who established Bryan's Station), and Andrew Ireland (he and I afterwards married sisters; Miss Luckey as you know), 22 in all and on the morning of September 22, 1779, we started for Kentucky with six horses, twelve milch cows and a bull.[33] The bull was my father's and being a good work animal we should need him in Kentucky. His burden for the journey was two large kettles we had used in making malt (my father having directed a part of his time in making malt). These kettles were strapped over a pack saddle on the bull's back—Boone, also, had two kettles used for ordinary purposes, which were strapped over one of the horses backs, and over the backs of the others were strapped various articles indispensable to our journey and to our wants after our arrival in Kentucky. And among other things were fire chopping axes, some cane hoes, a sifter and churn.[34] (The two last articles and the two family kettles were Mrs. Boone's.) Thus armed and equipped we began our journey all afoot except the women and small children, who were added to the other burdens of the horses. The parting from friends was sad, and it was not without an effort myself and brothers gave our mother the parting hand who wept as though her heart would break. All was well with us until we reached the Clinch River, over a better route, Boone said, than the old one. We reached it at noon the fourth day and found that a rain that had fallen the previous night had swollen the stream so that we could not, in safety, ford it. The next morning, though fordable, the women, some of them, were afraid to cross, when Jemima Boone, Daniel's oldest daughter, and who was a very brave and handsome girl of sixteen years, told her father to get ready and she would lead the way across the stream. Accordingly all got ready. John Dodson with Mrs. Boone and her child behind him and I with Mrs. Dickey behind me and Jemima Boone with Dodson's eight year old daughter behind her all plunged into the water and nearly reached the opposite bank when Jemima's horse became frightened at some floating drift and suddenly whirled and threw Jemima and the little girl head foremost into the stream. A loud scream went up from the women, but as quick as thought Dodson and I leaped into the water leaving the women behind us to make their way to shore. When we struck the water the two girls were out of sight under the water but immediately they came to the surface and we seized them and bare them to the shore. The little girl was badly strangled, but Jemima seemed to enjoy the misfortune. She and two of Colonel Callaway's daughters during the sojourn of her parents in Kentucky were captured by the Indians on July 14, 1776, whilst playing in a canoe on the Kentucky River near the fort and borne off, but the next day the enraged fathers overtook their captors, killed two of the five Indians and the others fled leaving their prisoners behind.[35] It was this narrow escape from a wretched fate that recurred to Jemima and led her to exclaim, when she reached shore—"A ducking is very disagreeable this chilly day but much less so than capture by the Indians."[36] This exclamation from the brave girl was responded to with a hearty laugh by the spectators.

The balance were soon over and we proceeded without incident worthy of note until we had completed a day's journey in Kentucky when, on the night of October 9 one of Boone's horses died.

This misfortune put the wits of Boone to work to devise a way to proceed with our burdens. But Boone, who was distinguished for always doing the right thing at the right time when confronted by difficulties was equal to the emergency on this occasion. He cut a small forked sapling, cut off the body near the fork, hewed the prongs thin and cut them off five feet long, beveled the fork upwards like a sled runner, cut three branches and notched them so as to fit tightly over the runners, passed bark around their ends and made them fast to the fork in front and then laid a floor on them of bark. He then put the four kettles on this floor and bound them all together with bark and placed the churn and meal sifter in one of the kettles. He then cut two crooked sticks for a bough[?], put them around the bull's neck and bound them, top and bottom, with bark. Then he made traces with bark, tied one to the bough on each side, ran them back with smooth sides to the bull and made them secure at the fork. He then cut a stretcher stick and fastened it behind the bull to the traces to keep them from chafing the bull's sides, and by this device (which he called a "truckle," and which, with wooden wheels added . . . common among the settlers) we had a horse liberated from the burden of Boone's two kettles for the accommodation of the women and children; the men and the boys having footed it all the way.

On October 11 we again started and found the bull perfectly at home behind his new out-fit, though inadvertently this burden had been increased. We had no further drawbacks until the 14th when Dodson's daughter, Jane, who had fallen in the water and was taken quite ill of measles, which detained us three days.

Meantime, some of the men were engaged in replenishing our culinary department with game which we found in abundance. The women baked Johnny cakes before our nightly fires and the men cooked the wild turkey and deer by running sharp sticks through slices of the meat and roasting it over the fire.[37] We thought we were living in luxury until we had exhausted the salt with which we started.

All slept in the open air with buffalo rugs for bedding except on unclear wet nights we constructed sheds of poles and bark. The little girl having passed the worst stages of her disease, we renewed our journey on the 17th; and on October 22, one month from the day we left old Squire Boone's, we arrived safely at the fort, and were received with rapturous delight by the old pioneer's friends. We found Squire Boone's wife and his youngest child—(Enoch, three years old and the first male white child born in Kentucky) very ill but they both recovered.[38]

There being no salt in the fort, Daniel on the 25th, took his brother, Ned, and some sacks and started, both on horseback, to the Lower Blue Licks where a company they thought was still making salt to sell.[39] On arriving they found the camp deserted and the kettles gone.

Being disappointed they retraced their journey. But a few miles after they had started they were fired on by Indians and Ned fell dead from his horse. The yell of the savages was interpreted by Boone to represent about twenty in number. Seeing his brother was dead he dashed off to save his own life and Ned's horse followed him. He arrived at home at ten o'clock at night and filled the fort with gloom. This was October 27, 1780.[40]

Early next morning, Daniel, at the head of 26 men, returned to bury Ned. They found him scalped and stripped of his clothing. They buried him, saw no Indians and returned to the fort. I will here correct an error into which the historian has been led (viz) that of saying it was Squire that was here killed. Some one, either from ignorance or through mistake started the tradition that it was Squire and the historian caught up the tradition and wrote it down and it became current history. There has no man lived whose opportunity to know the facts in the case was better than my own. I was in the fort when Daniel and his brother Ned started to the licks. I was there when Daniel returned. And Squire Boone was in the fort during their absence waiting on his sick family. And he was one of the 26 who went to bury his brother. And in the fall of 1790 he with his family moved to Boone's Station in Shelby County and at a later period sold out there and moved to Indian Creek, in what is now Lawrence County, Indiana, only 28 or thirty miles south of Bloomington, and his grandson Noah, son of Isaiah is living on the old homestead at this time.[41]

The fort still suffering for want of salt, Daniel concluded to go to Goose Creek salt springs, take his kettles and make some salt.[42] Accordingly, on October 29, Daniel hitched a horse to his "truckle" tied his two kettles on it that we had brought from North Carolina, took Isaiah Boone—Squire's son above named—Levy Dickey, James Blue and myself and started for the springs; Isaiah driving the horse and truckle, I and Daniel on a second horse, and Dickey and Blue on a third horse. The course was south east of Boonesborough and the distance three days travel. We arrived at the springs the night of November 1, lit our tinder (burnt rags in a close fitting tin box which was ignited by a piece of steel and a flint), made a fire and ate our suppers and slept until next morning.[43]

The 2nd of November was spent in boiling salt water and on the

3rd, Daniel started. Blue (who was well acquainted with the route) rode back to the fort with a small wallet of salt for the inhabitants. The balance of us remained until the 7th, boiling all the time through the day but always extinguishing our fire before dark lest it might be discovered by the Indians and they would come upon us . . . in the night. In the evening of the 7th, we had made over a bushel of salt and having left Ned's wife and child sick, Daniel was uneasy and had intended to start for the fort next morning, and had taken off the kettles from the fire and fastened them securely on the truckle and we were all sitting on a log discussing whether or not to travel a part of the way that night. The sun was about an hour high and whilst we were discussing, one of our horses lifted his head and looking up the creek, snorted fearfully. "There are Indians near!" whispered Boone. We all sprung to our feet and seized our rifles and got ready for the worst. But Boone told us all to be silent, and keep a sharp lookout. We could see from our hiding place about 120 yards up the creek to a turn it made in the direction the horses kept looking, with every few minutes, a snort. Finally we saw three Indians come into sight from around the bend. Again Boone gave us orders to be silent until he gave the word. The Indians continued to approach us, evidently knowing nothing of our presence. But having approached within about eighty yards of us they discovered the smoke from our fire and halted, all three of them got behind a large tree and began to peer out from behind it.

"Be silent," said Boone "until we see whether there are more behind." Ten minutes elapsed, I suppose, when, the Indians still peeping from their cover, two on one side and one on the other, when Boone ordered Dodson to draw a bead on the single Indian and for Dickey and I both to aim at "the tall Indian" and he would take the other. We all fired at the word "fire" from Boone. Boone's Indian and ours fell but Dodson's gun failed to go off and his Indian, with a terrific yell, took to the brush. We did not go to the dead Indians. They were both shot through the head for we could see no other part of them and they pitched forward and fell in full view.

Boone, fearing the escaped Indian might return with an overpowering force ordered us to "be quick and strap the kettles together," which we did by taking the bark they were tied on the truckle with by running the bark through the eyes of the kettles. Meantime, Boone had the horses in readiness with the sack of salt across one of their backs. And across this "pack saddle" the kettles were swung and two and two we mounted and off we started for the fort, traveled all night, changing, as we went, the kettles from one horse to the other as they were tired.

And frequently we all walked to rest the horses. We reached the fort on the night of November 9. We never visited the Goose Creek Springs again from the fort.

Immigrants continued to arrive and a want of wearing apparel and bed-clothes was felt, and Boone, to supply the want took me and my brothers, Andy Ireland, Levy Dickey with his two brothers George and Jonathan, and went to the mouth of what he, in honor of the Houston boys afterward named "Houston Creek" where it enters into Stoner Creek and where the town of Paris now stands. And about a hundred yards west of where Paris stands and on a bluff of Houston Creek we built a small fort, or station, sixteen feet square using logs for the walls and bark for a roof; hewing the logs—top and bottom, and notching them down tight together as a protection against an assault from the Indians.[44] Having completed the fort, Dickey and I returned to Boonesborough and swung the two malt kettles over the bull's back, took them to Houston fort where Boone had in readiness a furnace near the fort door to receive the kettles. The kettles were set and there we remained to watch the buffalo trail that passed near; but out of sight of the fort, and to kill buffalo and deer as they passed, take their hides and roll their carcasses into Houston Creek that they might be borne off by the water and not remain to frighten our game from the trail. The deer hides we tanned by heating water in the kettles, and making it strong with salt, alum and ashes (poor ingredients for tanning, but the best we had and they answered our purpose). And into this solution we placed the deer skins, having the water quite warm. In a day or two the hair was removed, the flesh side scraped and as the hides dried, they were constantly pulled and stretched. Of this, leather trousers and jackets and moccasins were made; principally for men but some of the women were under the necessity of wearing them.[45]

The buffalo hides we did not put into the kettles, but covered the flesh side with the solution made the consistency of paste and after a few days all the flesh was removed and the hides pulled and rubbed until they were dry. Of these we made bed quilts.

We remained at this business at Houston fort until we had supplied the wants of the immigrants. Meantime, returning to Boonesborough frequently as we learned rumors of danger, though we were never pestered by Indians during the eight months we were there. We completed our fort on November 16, 1780, and left there on July 18, 1781.

The titles to lands that had been sold by Henderson's Company having been declared invalid, and titles in general being endangered by the many grants and entering that had not been registered, Boone thought it unadvisable to locate me and my brothers until he was sure our title would be good accounts for our location at the Houston fort to tan hides for clothing. We received six shillings for each hide tanned. During our stay at fort Houston we hunted a great deal through what is now called Bourbon County, and I took a great liking to the land, and determined that when my brothers and I located it should be in that section and I so told Daniel and he concurred in my judgment.

The winter of 1780 being extremely cold—as cold, I think as any during my long life—the settlers were not annoyed by Indians.[46] But as early as March in 1781, they entered what is now Jefferson and Shelby Counties. They killed a number of the settlers by laying in ambush in Jefferson.[47] And in Shelby, whilst a colony established by Squire Boone at Squire Boone's Station, where Shelbyville now stands, were retreating to Bear's Creek Station for greater safety they were fired on and seven of them killed and the Indians put forth a yell of victory and fled.[48] Daniel and Squire hearing of this they immediately went with a party from Lexington to the rescue of the colony, but upon their arrival they learned that the Indians had left for Ohio.

They remained, however, until August enlarging and strengthening Fort Boone and doing all they could for the safety and comfort of the colony. It was the 13th day of August 1781 that they arrived again at Boonesborough where Daniel remained with his family and hunted with others to supply meat for the fort, and in meeting immigrants by the way, conducting them on to the fort and seeing to their comfort after their arrival. He was one of the most benevolent and fatherly men I ever knew, and all looked to him as their counselor and guide.

It was during this year—1781—that the colonies began to fear the two notorious traitors Simon Girty and Colonel Alexander McKee, especially the former who had earned the title of "Simon Girty the Savage," he having acquired all of the savage habits that renders the savage odious.[49] Repeatedly during the fall and winter the colonies received the intelligence that Simon Girty would invade Kentucky with a large army of Indians composed of various tribes with a view to exterminate the white settlements. This intelligence forewarned every settlement to put their forts in order, and to prepare for the worst, and we were not disappointed.

On the 15th day of August, 1782, a body of Indians stealthily appeared before Bryan's Station and made an attack upon it with rifles.[50] A few of the men were out in their field near by, and believing the long looked for Girty and his Indian army had arrived one of them started to

Mythic image of Girty, based on Edward Chatfield's Huron sketches or on 1880 Huron photographs by J. E. Livernois. Despite its late date and unknown provenance, this sketch—showing trade silver, wampum belt, finger-woven sash, peace medals, leggings, quilled strips, and gastoweh (feathercap)—correctly depicts the hybrid half-caste personae of Indian-influenced frontier whites.

Boonesborough to give the alarm, and one to Lexington. Having secured the intelligence, Boone from our fort started immediately for the seat of war taking with him all the men except sufficient to defend the fort. And Colonel Todd of Lexington notified Colonel Trigg at Harrodsburg and Colonel Benjamin Logan at Logan's Station.[51] Trigg, Todd and Boone all arrived at Bryan's next day in the evening to find the fort safe and the Indians gone, having killed no one in the fort, and wounded but four men, nor is it known that over a half dozen Indians were killed. They shot from a distance and from behind trees, and attempted to fire the back roof by shooting burning arrows, but failed.[52]

A council of war was held. Boone was asked his opinion as to the propriety of pursuing the Indians at once or await the arrival of Colonel Logan who had sent a message to Colonel Todd that he would be at the fort on the evening of the 18th. Boone having examined the camp of the Indians and its surrounding signs had formed the conclusion that not more than forty or fifty Indians had occupied the camp. That they had been sent forward by Girty as a decoy. Knowing that after the assault and retreat they would be pursued as usual by the colonists and that Girty was some where on the line of retreat with a large force ready to assail the pursuing colonists by surprise, and therefore his judgment was that they await the arrival of Colonel Logan. But so impetuous were the feelings of Majors McGary and Harlan that Boone's counsel was not heeded.[53] And early the next morning—August 19, 1782—one hundred and eighty two men, old and young, my self and my brother Robert, among them, started with dispatch on the trail of the Indians.

And as we were all on horseback we arrived at the Blue Lick about two o'clock, a distance of about thirty six miles.

Having arrived at the ford and being satisfied the Indians had crossed the Licking, Boone appealed to Colonel Todd to call a halt and hold a council which he did, though Majors McGary and Harlan who neither of them had any experience in Indian warfare, opposed the halt and the council.

Here Boone told the Colonels that as they had advanced he had noticed that an effort had been made by the Indians to make their retreating trail so distinct, that their pursuers could not miss it, and that his experience was that Indians never did this, but the reverse unless they desired to be pursued—hoping to get advantage of their pursuers by concealing themselves in ambush—that he was certain therefore, the Indians they were pursuing were in ambush not far distant, and, as he believed, not more than a mile beyond the river. And just at this time two Indians made their appearance over the river on the ridge which we were to traverse should we cross. The Indians stared at us for a few minutes then turned and leisurely retreated. The appearance of the two Indians and their tardy retreat was interpreted by Boone as an additional proof that Todd and his men were being decoyed and then he proposed that the Colonel should await the arrival of Colonel Logan; but the two Majors and others from Lexington opposed it saying, "We have force enough to whip all the Indians we will find." Boone then told them if they were determined to proceed that they should cross the river and divide. Colonel Todd to command one division and Colonel Trigg the other and march one to the left and the other to the right in the "horse-shoe" made by a curve of the river with the toe of the shoe at the ford, and near the heels of the shoe Boone believed the Indians were secreted in two ravines, running from opposite directions and extending to near the top of the ridge running through the center of the shoe from toe to heels and on top of which lay the road with all of which Boone had, previously become well acquainted. After hearing Boone, Todd was decidedly in favor of awaiting the arrival of Colonel Logan who had much more experience in Indian warfare than he or any other officer in his command. But McGary and Harlan became impatient at the detention of Boone's council, and being that Todd was swayed by Boone, McGary flourished his hand in the air, wheeled his horse for the ford and cried out—"All that are not cowards follow me" and the enthusiastic young men followed him. Boone appealed to Todd, who was commander in chief—to assert his authority and stop the procedure but he replied, "Let them go, and we will remain in the rear, and if they are surprised by the Indians the blame will be on McGary and he will have the brunt to bear."[54] My brother and I and Daniel's son, Israel, and his brother, Samuel, kept near to Boone having more faith in him to get us out of trouble should we get in than in of the officers. We all followed—the Lexington troops, principally, went to McGary, the Harrodsburg troops next; and we of Boonesborough in the rear and had proceeded until the front had passed the ravines and reached the woods covered with underbrush just beyond, whilst the middle division . . . yet between the ravines and our division close up, but not having entered between the ravines; when suddenly in front of the first division a terrific war whoop was heard, which was caught up all along the ravines on both sides, proving that a gauntlet had been formed for us to run and that the body of Indians in front had been stationed there to keep us from getting out in that direction. Simultaneously with the yell, the rifles began a terrific fire. Boone at once took in the hopeless situation and cried aloud to Colonel Todd, who with Trigg were isolated a little to our right, "Colonel Todd, order a retreat across the river and make your fight there, the Indians are surrounding you." But before Todd could accomplish anything he and Colonel Trigg both fell amid a shower of bullets from the ravine on the right. But McGary needed no order to retreat. His men, having emptied their guns, and seeing the Indians swarming from the woods in front, and having no time to reload, he whirled and began a rapid retreat leaving one third of his division sweltering in blood with Major Harlan among them. Meantime, Boone and his division not having got into the gauntlet he cried out to them—"hold your fire recross the river and hold the Indians at bay until our men have crossed." This order was obeyed, we recrossed and Ben Netherland, a brave man, repeated the order of Boone as soon as he had crossed saying to all as they landed, "Stand and fire on the Indians and give our men a chance to cross the river." They obeyed and doubtless more Indians were killed as they descended the hill to the ford than were killed on the field of battle. The ridge where our men were fired on was almost barren and they were exposed whilst the Indians were protected by trees in front and by bushes in the ravines, and my impression is that but few Indians were killed by the emptying of our guns. Had the Indians rushed to the edge of the brush and timber before they fired they might have killed all the advance, and all that were in the gauntlet. But, as we saw when we returned to bury our dead, a great many of their balls had struck the trees and bushes before they passed out of the hiding places. They evidently, most of them, emptied their guns in the assault, and then began to close in on our men intending to complete their work with spears and tomahawks. Myself and my brother Robert were in front of Boone and his son and did not miss them until we had recrossed the river, but in a few minutes Boone's nephew, Samuel, crossed, wounded in the leg and told us that Israel Boone had been shot from his horse and that Daniel had dismounted to bring him away before him on his own horse and he expected his uncle had been killed also. But by the time our men yet living had all crossed, we saw a man plunge into the river some seventy-five yards below. He swam across, and it proved to be Daniel Boone, who came up and mounted in front of his nephew, and told us, that when his son Israel fell, shot through the neck, he leaped from his horse, intending to take him on his horse before him, but his horse pulled from him, and followed the other horses that were rapidly passing with their riders. "I called to our fleeing men for help but they heeded not; whereupon I took my boy on my shoulder, and with gun in hand I hastened for the bushes on the bluff. Three Indians discovered me, and with a yell pursued me into the bushes. A very large Indian was ten steps in advance of the others and with my son on my shoulders, I saw I would soon be overtaken, and was forced to abandon my son. I let him to the ground, raised my gun and the big Indian fell, then, being, familiar with the country, I found no trouble in eluding pursuit of the other Indians and here I am safe, thank God, but it is painful to think that my poor boy has fallen prey to the scalping knife."[55] And here the grand old pioneer wept bitterly.

I saw but few horsemen among the Indians. Had they been on horseback the result would have been much more disastrous. Some of the Indians started into the water, and even scalped a few of our men who had lost their horses and become exhausted, and some of them wounded, but they knew it would be useless to pursue us further on foot.

We all returned, who were alive, to Bryan's, and met Colonel Logan a few miles before we reached it coming to our aid. I understood his force consisted of near three hundred men, but even had his force been with us and we had followed the impetuous McGary the result would have been the same.[56] Never was there an army better prepared to deal death to their enemies with less harm to themselves than was the army of Indians we met; never was an army in a more helpless condition than ours on this occasion. We have never been able to learn the numbers of the Indians; but taking the yells and the reports of their rifles for a guide with their appearance when they come . . . the open field they could not have been much short of five hundred.[57] In an open field, our force with Logan's would have been an over match for them, but with their ambush to protect them they could have vanquished a thousand men.

After getting reports from all of our divisions we were out seventy-three men—sixty-seven of whom we thought were killed and the other six taken prisoners. Though, as Boone said, "There is no good reason for believing any were taken prisoners."[58]

The next day, August 20th, Logan and his force joined the other forces and proceeded to the Lick to bury the dead and to retaliate on the Indians if found, but none were found and but forty-six of the dead bodies of our comrades were found and buried.[59] Boone found the body of his son where he had left it in the thicket. Its locality was all the proof he had that he had found the body of poor Israel. The body had been stripped of its clothing and scalped and partly devoured by wild beasts, and all the rest that were found were in like condition. No dead Indians were found nor any Indian graves. The same night we returned and next morning the soldiers were dismissed at Bryan's Station.

But by September 22, only thirty days from this disbandment, General Clark, residing at the Falls, had called for, and, under Colonels Floyd, Boone, and Logan, had enlisted one thousand men, and from the mouth of the Licking River started, on that day for Chillicothe, Ohio, to retaliate on the Indians. And the historian tells you, that although the Indians were apprised of his approach and fled, still he spread devastation and ruin, not only over Chillicothe but over every village throughout their country, sparing neither towns nor wigwams nor a vestige of any thing upon which the savages could subsist.[60] This raid with the close of the Revolutionary War gave a quietus to Indian raids into Kentucky except by marauding bands. We were all quiet again and Boone was more hopeful than at any period since the establishment of Boonesborough.

The commissioners appointed by the Governor of Virginia to examine and settle conflicting and doubtful land claims had spent several months at Boonesborough for the benefit of disputants in our section and had, on the 9th day of March 1781, adjourned without completing their work. And by the hostilities of the Indians the commissioners were prevented from reassembling until December 4, 1782. Boone's claim to a tract of land, on which he had erected a comfortable house and which he claimed, not by purchase or preemption but by "right of discovery" had been postponed at the former session, as had his claim under Henderson as a gift for services performed.[61] The commissioners having met, Boone's claims, by his counsel were presented and pressed with great force: the counsel relying on the great services Boone had rendered the state as its first successful pioneer to excite the sympathies of the commissioners, and influence them to grant Boone's claims but all in vain. They read the law and told the counsel that whilst the case of Boone was one to excite sympathy, yet many were equally unfortunate and that the law was inexorable. But they advised Boone to appeal to the Legislature for help, which he afterwards did, but without avail. Congressmen, however, were appealed to after he left the state and a tract of land was given him in Missouri, after he moved to that state, it containing 850 acres not far from where St. Louis now stands.[62]

Having now learned that the lands lying between Stoner and Hinkston Creeks were free from claims, and Boone thinking it would be safe to locate me and my brothers, he and John Longnecker, Andy Ireland, Michael Stoner, my two brothers and myself started on March 3, 1783, for what is now Bourbon County, and for several days hunted and explored the country from Houston Station up Stoner Creek on both sides. Stoner concluded to buy and locate on Stoner Creek about halfway between where Paris and North Middletown are now located and immediately on the road that now connects the two towns above named.[63] Longnecker, Ireland and the Houston boys chose to locate about five miles northeast of Stoner's selection at the location dividing the waters of Hinkston and Stoner Creeks and about two miles north of where North Middletown now stands.

Having effected our purchases, we, the Houston boys, the first day of April returned from Boonesborough to our land. The three men

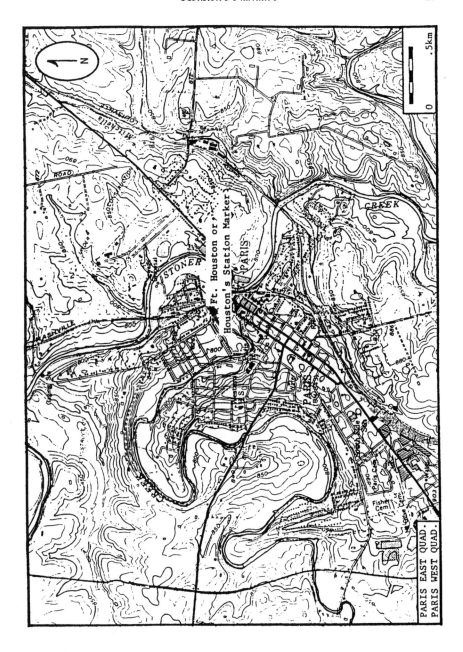

Plat of Houston's Station (Courtesy Nancy O'Malley, from *Stockading Up: A Study of Pioneer Stations in the Inner Bluegrass Region of Kentucky*, 1987, Archaeological Report 127, Department of Archaeology, University of Kentucky, Lexington.)

above named with us. We soon threw up the first log cabin within a range of five miles, in which to lodge at night and rest from our labors of clearing ground. We then repaired to Stoner's purchase and built a cabin for him, Boone, as was his habit, taking the lead and having everything his own way. Longnecker and Ireland did not build and move to the neighborhood for three years afterwards. In that year, 1786, I and Ireland returned to North Carolina and married sisters, Katy and Molly Luckey, two of our old schoolmates.

We stopped on our return at Boonesborough, saw Boone and his family and they promised to come to see me and my young wife in a few days. And on October 14, 1786, just one month after I was married he and his wife complied with their promise. They remained with us three weeks and Boone having found me with logs ready to put up a malt house he engineered that and saw it completed and the two big kettles set that the bull had drawn from North Carolina, and which we had left at Houston Station where we had used them in tanning. We took several hunts whilst he was with us, and on one occasion we went to Stoner Creek in search of wild turkeys and having killed three, he two of them, he took me to a spring running out of one of the banks of Stoner Creek to slake our thirst, and when we arrived, he looked at the gurgling water for a moment as if deterred from drinking, but presently said, "Peter, here is a spring that John Findley and I and my brother Squire often visited during our first visit to Kentucky."[64]

We drank and sat down to rest and he related many reminiscences of his first visit to Kentucky. The conversation led to moral questions, and these to questions of religion. His family were what was called Friends and I was, then, a Presbyterian and we got into a sharp discussion of the relative merits of our creeds.[65] And the dispute became so sharp that Boone, after a short silence in a reflecting mood looked at me and said, "Peter I never knew any good to come of religious disputes and I want to make an agreement with you that we will never dispute again on the subject of religion." I agreed to it and we shouldered our turkeys and moved off pleasantly together for home. And when we arrived he insisted that he could "beat anybody picking and dressing turkeys" and not a soul would he let take a part in dressing those turkeys. And then he said he would show my wife how to cook one for supper. He tied a piece of bark to the neck and hung it before the fire and called for a pewter plate (all the kind the colonies used then) to set under it to catch the gravy. And with a pewter spoon he continued to dip the gravy and pour it over the turkey and at the same time keeping the turkey turning round and round until it was thoroughly roasted.

And at supper, it appeared that he not only knew how to cook a turkey, but to eat it as well.

But Daniel's visit, which up to the 29th of October had been enjoyed very much by us all, was turned into sadness that day. A few days previous Daniel's brother Ned had also come to make us a visit, and on the 29th he and Daniel started to a spring four miles northeast of our cabin on a creek which ever after this day was called Boone's Creek in honor of Ned Boone, who, on that day was killed at the spring running out of its bed.[66] When the creek was dry, which was the case of this occasion, this spring afforded water for wild beasts and to which they resorted for water, as the Boones had long since learned and at which they had previously killed deer and other game. In the evening Daniel returned alone and stated as following: "We halted about eighty yards before we reached the spring and secreted ourselves to watch for game. We had waited near three hours without seeing any game when Ned with gun in hand, went to the spring to get a drink. And whilst upon his hands and knees drinking several shots were fired at him from a thicket surrounding a large hickory tree about seventy yards beyond the spring from me and I saw Ned spring backwardly and fall. A yell from seven Indians immediately followed the reports of the guns as they dashed from the bushes and ran towards my brother. I saw at once my brother was dead and that an attempt to rescue his body would be but a sacrifice of my own life. But I determined if possible to get two of the Indians in range whilst they were scalping him and stripping him of his clothes (which I knew they would do). It was several minutes before I got two of the Indians in range—and not then satisfactorily—but time was precious and I fired killing the Indian next to me and so badly wounding the other that he went crippling after the others who fled towards the thicket from whence they had come. Amid their confusion I made my escape." And then he wept.

During the two years previous, several families had settled near us. We raised ten men with tools to dig a grave and proceeded next morning to the spring, found the body stripped and scalped and buried it under a buckeye tree near where they had secreted themselves and on the side of the tree next to the grass, Daniel cut the letters "N Boone."[67] We returned without seeing the Indians. Such events were still common and continued for several years, being perpetrated by scouts of Indians.

Having remained with me three weeks Daniel returned to Boone's Station, determined to make an appeal to the legislature to reinstate him with his old home upon which he settled his family when he first arrived to Kentucky.

Daniel having returned to Boone's Station, he was appointed about the 15th of November, 1786, with four others to go to Limestone (now Maysville) to form a treaty with the western Indian chiefs for exchange of prisoners.[68]

The treaty was entered into at Limestone and under it quite a number of prisoners were exchanged. And no small proportion of them were women and girls.[69]

As Daniel returned from Limestone he stopped and tarried with me a day and night (November 26, 1786) and this was the last I saw of him until March 8, 1789. With him on that day was his wife and his son Nathan (who was the youngest of his nine children).[70]

Daniel, who with my brother Robert and ten others went to Missouri in 1799 to trap beaver, and Nathan who was a little over five months old when we all left Yadkin for Kentucky and whose birthday was the day he and his parents arrived at my house as above stated.[71] And when his mother spoke of the fact my wife, with Mrs. Boone to help her prepared for the boy and the rest of us a very good pioneer dinner and a part of which was a good fat opossum. And upon that Daniel feasted most bountifully.

After Daniel with his wife and son had been welcomed into my cabin and whilst he still held my hand he said: "Well, Peter I have concluded to leave Kentucky and I thought before I started I would visit as many as possible of my old friends and bid them a final adieu."[72]

"Why," said I, "where in the world are you going and what for?"

"Well," he said, "I am first going to the land of my birth and take a last look on all that remains there with which I was familiar in my boyhood. And from there I will go to some point beyond the bounds of civilization and spend the remnant of my days in the woods. I have lived to learn that your boasted civilization is nothing more than improved ways to overreach your neighbor. I came to Kentucky as a woodsman but having a wife and a large family of children whom I loved and desiring they should enjoy the advantages of civilization I done what I could to subdue the forest, drive out the untamable Indian and to encourage and assist immigration in every way within my power. And for all my privations and toils I thought I was entitled to a home for my family without further cost. Accordingly near Boonesborough, as you well know, I selected a tract of land and upon it erected a comfortable house for myself and family, and there expected to enjoy the advantages of civilization; but another bought the land over my head and bade me go way, which I refused to do, and I appealed my case to the Governor and I rcccivcd in response a set of Commissioners who, after hearing my story told me that I held my home without legal sanction and that I must vacate it. Now Peter, I always thought that civilization carried with it sympathy, gratitude and justice but I find that no one of these has been exhibited in my case, and I am, therefore, soured against civilization."[73]

I was deeply touched by this plaintive story. Knowing as I did that the grounds for it were more than ample, but I endeavored to console him by telling him that if the state had proved ungrateful, his friends would stand by him and see that, in the end, his services were recognized and compensated.

The next morning I went with him to see Thomas Starks, another of his old North Carolina friends who had located two years previous a short distance northwest of me. We took hickory bark with us to torch us back, intending to tarry until bed-time. But so interested did we become in the hair-lifting stories of Boone that it must have been long after midnight before we had lighted our torch and started. The cane was thick and high with a narrow path cut from house to house.[74] And as we plodded along Boone remarked, "Peter, I think this ridge is more densely covered with cane than any other section I have found in Kentucky and for this reason Squire and I and Findley called it 'Cane Ridge' whilst we were hunting here during my first visit to Kentucky."

And from that day to this the ridge has been called Cane Ridge. We had reached within a quarter of a mile of home when we were startled by the hideous scream of a panther. (I should have said at the proper time that Starks had given us a ham of fresh deer for our dinners the next day when he and his wife were to be with us.) The panther had scented the ham of deer and was in pursuit of it.

We hastened but the wall of cane on either side soon knocked our torch to pieces and we were left with nothing but the walls of cane to guide us. Thrice the scream was heard the last time very near us whilst we were yet two hundred yards from the house when Boone said, "Peter we will have to leave our meat or we shall soon be overtaken," and down he threw it. We heard no more of the panther; he had found what he was after. And as soon as we reached the house I ran to my kennel and let out Nip and Tuck, two ferocious Spaniel dogs for hunting. They had heard the panther and were howling at a fearful rate to get after it. I gave them the direction and off they went. Boone and I and his son Nathan, who had sprung out of bed, awaiting the result. It was well nigh a half hour before we heard the dogs bay.

"There," said I "they have treed him."

"Well," said Boone "let us get our guns and tinder box and go after him." (The tinder box was a small box in which the settlers burned cotton cloth to tinders—nearly ashes—and fit a top over it to shut out moisture. And when a fire was wanted thin dry shavings were prepared, the top of the box removed and by the friction of a flint and piece of steel sparks were thrown upon the tinder which took fire and the shavings were ignited. Sometimes powder, when plentiful, was used for tinder.)[75] I remonstrated against going a mile through the cane at that late hour to kill the panther. But Boone said, "no panther shall run me and rob me of my dinner without value received. If you do not want to go I will go alone." So I yielded. Nathan was anxious to go with us but his mother forbade it. It was near on an hour before we completed our struggle through the cane and reached the dogs, who kept us posted as to their location by their yelps. The tree was a leaning oak. We halted some thirty yards from the tree and Boone said "light your shavings behind me so that I can see his eyes plainly." The light was struck and the fiery eyes of the panther were visible to Boone. He leveled his gun, fired and down came one of the largest panthers my eyes ever beheld, though Boone said "I have killed many such." No sport was left for Nip and Tuck: Boone, without being able to use the sights on his gun, had struck the panther almost squarely between the eyes.

On the morning of the 12th, my old friend and benefactor was ready to shake my hand as I verily believed for the last time and it was all that I could do to bear up under my weight of grief. Knowing as I did that aside from my parents I was about to bid adieu forever to the best friend I had on earth.[76]

"Hold your hand," said I to Boone. "You tell me you owe a few little debts and have no money to supply your wants on your long journey, and that you are troubled much about it. Here is two pounds sterling, all I have by me, it will help you on your journey."

Instead of receiving the money he threw both his arms around my neck and wept like a child, and his wife joined with him in tears. It was quite awhile before he sufficiently recovered himself to speak and when he had he said, "No Peter, my kind-hearted friend, you must excuse me. I cannot accept of your kindness in money. You are just beginning life and you will need your money, I have lived this long by the help of my gun and my trusty old rifle will not desert me hereafter in the hour of need." And with all my pleadings I could not prevail on him to accept my proffered aid. But I was determined it should not end thus and whilst Daniel and his son were leading up their horses that were tied in the cane near by I turned to his wife and said, "Aunt Rebecca, your husband has refused to take this money. You must take it, otherwise I shall think you have no respect for me."

"Well Peter, my feelings are with the decision of Mr. Boone but rather than have you think that I do not respect you as my own child I must accept it." And again she gave way to tears. Daniel knew nothing of this but learned it afterward as the sequel will show.

They left my house to go straight to Yadkin and from there to his old native home. They had two horses; Rebecca and her son rode one and on her saddle there were two buffalo rugs and hanging on the horn of her saddle was a deer skin satchel filled with wearing apparel, whilst Boone, also, had two buffalo rugs on his saddle and his gun on his shoulder and his shot pouch around his neck.

How sad my wife and I felt as those three souls grew dim in the distance. He had been my Kentucky father, and she had been my Kentucky mother, and the dear boy, how many miles had I carried him in my arm to rest his mother as we trudged our way in the fall of 1780 from the old North State to this wilderness land. And now to see them driven by ingratitude from their adopted state to seek a home in their old days beyond the borders of civilization was crushing to my feelings. My eyes followed them along the path through the cane until they disappeared. I then sat down upon a stump and wept. Years rolled away and I never heard from Boone again until in 1795—six years after he left my house the last time. Several of our colonists from Boonesborough were at Limestone (now Maysville) and there saw Boone, his wife and son on their way to Missouri.[77]

But in the summer of 1802, June 3rd I was out at my little stable feeding a few pigs I had to keep in a strong pen to save them from wild beasts, and I saw, at about three o'clock in the evening, a man coming up afoot leading a black horse with buffalo rugs tied on his saddles. I gazed at him until he had gotten within thirty steps of me when his walk reminded me of Boone and I soon decided from his walk that it must be Boone, and not willing to remain longer in suspense, I cried out at the top of my voice: "Is that Daniel Boone?" The reply was, "O my boy I am glad to see you." This was enough, I ran to meet him and once again we were in each other's arms.

I will not enter into details of his life during the thirteen years of his absence. He went from my house to his people in the Yadkin, thence to the place of his birth in Pennsylvania. Thence to the mouth of the Kanawha River on the Ohio River and after remaining there until 1799 he went to Missouri by Limestone and the Falls, stopping several days at each place, and in September of that year reached his son Daniel

Morgan who was trapping on the Missouri and Mississippi Rivers, and joined him in the trapping business; selling their furs to a company stationed where St. Louis now stands.

They made money at trapping, and the old pioneer—as he had said he would do if God spared him—had now returned to Kentucky in his old age "to pay those little debts that have all the time troubled me" to use his own language to me on the day of his arrival at my house.[78]

He remained with me one week, and on the morning of the 10th he said, as he approached me, "Well Peter, I have settled with all but you and here are the two pounds you forced upon my wife and one pound for interest."

I replied, "upon my word I will not take it." He then turned to my wife and said, "Molly, I justly owe your husband this money and you see he has positively refused to take it. You, then, must take it, and if you do not I shall leave you believing you have lost all respect for me."

"Oh, Uncle Boone," she replied, "do not insist on having me to accept your money so much against my will." "I must insist and I will take no denial," he continued.

"Well," said Molly "If nothing else will do I will have to accept the two lbs. but the interest I cannot, will not accept."

"Very well," said Boone and he counted out the forty shillings and then stepped to our cradle in which was laying our little Enoch four months old and named for Squire Boone's son Enoch who was born in the fort at Boonesborough, and was the first white male child born in Kentucky. And as he looked the child in the face he lifted his right hand above his head and said: "My dear helpless innocent little child may God preserve your life and keep you from harm, and may you grow up an honor to your parents and a benefactor of your race, and as proof of the sincerity of my prayer I will crown your bosom with twenty shillings," and down he laid them. And once more and certainly for the last time he gave us the parting hand, and started upon his long journey to the wilderness of Missouri to join his sons in his favorite occupation of trapping and hunting for a livelihood.[79]

In appearance Boone was muscular and tall and as straight as an Indian. His hair was black, his eye was dark and peered out from beneath his projecting brow like the eye of an eagle. He was dark complected with features that always attracted the attention of the stranger.[80]

I think, that at the end of a hand spike he could lift more than any man I ever saw. At log-rolling and house-raisings he was always leader and director. He was forbearing with enemies but when nothing but

hostile blows would do he administered them freely and victoriously—
as the Indians often learned to their sorrow.

Kentucky has never yet appreciated the services of Daniel Boone
the old pioneer of Kentucky. A thousand years from now when the historian looks back over the dark blue sea of time for the origin of Kentucky's greatness he will find it in the adventurous spirit and
indomitable will of Boone the pioneer.

And what did Kentucky do for him whilst living? Nothing! And
what has she done for his memory since dead? Nothing! True, she is
now talking of removing his remains from Missouri to Frankfort and
erecting a monument over them but a tribute to the memory of a benefactor dead is a poor recompense for ingratitude to a benefactor living.[81]

I have now given you a sketch of the life and character of my old
friend and benefactor Daniel Boone who by his good neighborship and
fatherly counsel to me brought me under lasting obligations to him. In
writing the foregoing sketch I have in the main, avoided detail. Had I
written all that I know about Daniel Boone I should have consumed
several reams of paper. I have endeavored to correct mistakes made by
the historians in what they have written. And to give a number of facts
and incidents of which they have said nothing, all of which I hope you
will find to be interesting.

May the Lord protect and prosper you is the prayer of your Grandfather.

Peter Houston

Appendix

The following documents consist mostly of letters exchanged between Peter Houston and his grandson, F. W. Houston. These notes help amplify the origin of Houston's long-lost Boone sketch, its fragile history, and show the singular efforts exerted by F. W. Houston in his attempts to preserve his grandfather's memoir. Of special note is the inclusion of Theodore O'Hara's poem "The Old Pioneer, Daniel Boone," which F. W. sent to Dr. Lyman C. Draper in 1887.

A

Letter to Dr. Lyman C. Draper from F. W. Houston, DM 20C:83.

North Middletown, Ky
November 14, 1887

Lyman C. Draper
Madison, Wisconsin
Dear Sir:

I have delayed answering your letter of inquiry hoping to obtain a sketch of my grandfather's life written by him fifty years ago and which I frequently . . . during the years 39 and 40 whilst attending Indiana State University located at Bloomington that state and to which place my grandfather removed from this country in 1825. The sketch was in manuscript and was in book form and at his death in 1854 fell into the hands of his youngest son Alfred, and at his death into the hands of his children. But the sketch disappeared by some unknown hand and cannot be found. [On July 4, 1895, F. W. wrote that the book of Houston family history here referred to had been destroyed by family members, as the deerhide-covered book was "so mutilated and the chirography so much obliterated." Family tradition says that a Houston descendent threw the tattered manuscript in a fire.]

However, in 1842 William Falls Thornton, a young lawyer of Paris, contemplated writing a biography of Boone and appealed to me for assistance and I immediately wrote to my grandfather requesting him to give me a sketch of the life and character of Daniel Boone so far as he was personally acquainted with him. He complied with my request and I gave a copy of his sketch to William Thornton and kept the original as a souvenir. Thornton died soon and the biography never appeared. And I will now give you a copy of the original which is still in my possession. It reads as follows—

Bloomington, Indiana
May 2, 1842

My highly esteemed grandson, your letter of recent date in behalf of William Falls Thornton who seeks for information relating to the life and character of Daniel Boone was duly received and my answer is as follows:

[At this point, Peter Houston began writing his Boone sketch.]

B

Peter Houston's addendum to Boone sketch, sent to F. W. Houston in May 1842. Found in DM 20C:84(66)-85.

P.S. When Boone and his wife visited me in 1799 to bid Molly and I farewell he gave me the churn and one of the kettles we brought from the Yadkin on the truckle and I went after them to Boonesborough. I brought them with me in 1825 when I moved to Bloomington, Indiana, where I am now living. The sifter and the other kettle he gave to Isaiah Boone, son of Squire Boone, who took them with him to Indian Creek Indiana when he and his father's family moved there and I suppose his children still have them. A tree fell on my kettle in my furnace whilst making sugar and broke it but the churn I have yet and shall keep it as long as I live in remembrance of my old friend and to remind me of the irksome journey from North Carolina to Kentucky and its association with the two kettles we took to Goose Creek where the three Indians came upon us.

Peter Houston

C

Undated addendum by F. W. Houston to Dr. Draper, DM 20C:85-86.

I have often seen the churn and have churned butter in it. After my grandfather's death it fell to his son Alfred and since Alfred's death I do not know who has it, but it was held only as a keep-sake long before Alfred died.

The other kettle and the sifter given to Isaiah Boone, fell into the hands of his son Noah, and at his death they became the property of his son Daniel Boone who married my oldest daughter, Nannie, in 180[?].

They now live in Bedford Indiana ten miles from Indian Creek where the father, grandfather and great grand father Squire Boone lived and died. My daughter and her husband, Daniel Boone, still have the kettle and the sifter, and have recently laid them carefully away as souvenirs. I have often seen these reminders of the days and people of long ago. One hundred and seven years ago the 22nd of last September these articles were borne through the wilderness from "the old North State." And what their history was previous to that time no mortal can tell. The kettles held each twenty gallons; the sifter is a board half inch thick bent to a circle, overlapped and riveted together with brass rivets. The bottom is woven of brass wire and apparently as sound as when put together. The rim is worn thin by use, around the top, and no wonder considering the number of generations it has served. Daniel prizes these rivets of the "ancient Boones" very highly, and no reasonable amount of money would separate him from them. He has quit using them and has laid them securely away.

In the materials sent you I hope you may find some things to aid you in writing a deserved and much needed biography of the renowned Boone, and in this hope, and in hope of a happy hereafter for you and I, I am

Very Truly Yours
F. W. Houston

D

This note written by Dr. Draper is in the upper right-hand margin of DM 20C:86.

F. W. Houston sent with this narrative two letters of Colonel G.T. Wilcox, of Eden, Jefferson County, Kentucky, dated October 7th & 28th, 1887—which I have placed with Colonel Wilcox's letters to me among the Squire Boone Papers. He also sent a copy of Col. Theodore O'Hara's dirge on Daniel Boone—which appears in Collins' <u>History of Kentucky</u>, volume 1, 591. L. C. D.

E

Letter to Dr. Draper from F. W. Houston, DM 20C:88-88(5).

Paris, Kentucky
November 2, 1887

Lyman C. Draper
Madison, Wisconsin
Dear Sir:

I am in this city en route south, hoping there to get relief from neuralgia. And as I came through North Middletown last evening I read your letter reminding me of my promise to furnish some incidents on the life of Daniel Boone. I had, two or three days previous, mailed to your address a copy of a "Sketch of Boone" by my grandfather Peter Houston which I hope, you have received ere this.

I suppose I should have stated in my . . . of the copy that the original manuscript having been written in bad ink, and having been subjected to the ravages of forty five years, is very much . . .; in fact quite a number of words and a few sentences with some figures I found entirely illegible, and whilst I could not expect to replace the missing words I endeavored to use such as I thought would convey his ideas. For instance the surname Boone was plain in the account of the killing on Boone's Creek, but the given name, with some other words, was obliterated, and whilst my own recollection was that it was Edwin or Edward, I found several traditions differing when I went to where the scene occurred. One had it "Ed," another Edward, another John, and several had it Jonathan. And as this name had the preponderance in its favor I finally gave it in the copy after having written it Edward.

Also in the account of Boone's return to Kentucky to liquidate his debts it was impossible to determine the date or year with certainty. But as it had more the appearance of 1802 I believe I put it down so. There were, also sentences in the account of the Blue Licks battle that I was forced to guess at. Also the years of Boone and my grandfather's departure from the Yadkin I was not able to make out, and having lost my library a few years since, by fire I had no authors at hand to consult, except Abbott's biography of Boone. He was of New Haven, Connecticut, and his biography of Boone was published in 1872 by Dodd and Mead office librarian of Congress—This author on page 230 says, "It was in the autumn of 1780 that Boone with his family returned to Boonesborough." Supposing that W. Abbott here gives the proper date I so supplied the illegible date.

I have not read a biography of Boone since I was a young man, and from what I then read I arrived at the conclusion that the difficulty of getting facts and incidents relating to the early history of Boone or of facts of any . . . was similar to the difficulties of the judges and jury getting facts in many cases of murder. Eye witnesses will give facts and versions greatly differing from each other; owing to the occupying different shared points, and having different degrees of candor in relating what they really saw.

You having informed me that you had long been gathering materials for a biography of Boone you will, in all probability, discover some inaccuracies in the sketch I have sent you, for although my grandfather was, unquestionably a good Christian man, and possessed, also a remarkable memory—especially as to all historical matters relating to Christianity and the Church yet, from the vast amount of his information it would not be a matter of . . . should his account of facts be, in some instances, disagreeing with well attested facts and that the fault be in his memory.

As to Boone's return to Kentucky to pay off his old debts it will not be out of place for me to relate a statement made to me by Joseph Trotter who lived and died some four miles north of Cane Ridge meeting house. I helped him to plant his corn in 1834 and whilst with him he repeatedly talked to me about Daniel Boone. Daniel had contracted a small debt with Joseph's father before he left Kentucky and when Boone returned to Kentucky the old man Trotter was dead, but Joseph told me that Boone hunted him up came to his house and made known to him that his business was to pay to him a debt due his father. Joseph knew nothing of the debt and so told Boone, and that he would give it to him whatever it was. Boone's reply was "I have come here to pay my debts and I will not leave here indebted to any man," and Joseph had to take the money.

Trotter told me, also, that there was a leaning oak tree still standing near a lick on Brush Creek that was notched some thirty feet from the ground, that his father had shown him, and told him it was done by Daniel Boone and that this tree in the branches of it, was a favorite resort of Boone for killing game.

But I find I am growing tedious. Hoping that you may live to give to the world a more reliable, and more desirable biography of the old pioneer than any that have yet appeared and that you may be amply rewarded for your labors, I am

Very Truly Yours,
F. W. Houston

F

Letter to Dr. Draper from F. W. Houston reporting the theft of the original Houston Boone memoir, DM 20C:89-89(1).

North Middlctown, Ky
December 12, 1887

Lyman C. Draper
Madison, Wisconsin
Dear Sir:

When I wrote to you from Paris I expected to be absent some time, but there meeting with a mishap the loss of some manuscripts (explained further in the accompanying notice) I remained and made an effort to recover them. Meantime whilst I was waiting and suffering from neuralgia a friend addressed me to apply for relief to a homeo-path—Dr. Vincent—and I did so, and having obtained some relief I concluded to return home and await the result of his prescription; not having heard however of the missing documents. And knowing now, that they were stolen from my buggy, and that the thief is not likely to risk detection for the sake of the reward my hope of recovering them is weak.

On arriving at home I found the books and letter sent by you to my address. For the books you will please accept my thanks. From a glance at their contents I feel assured that their perusal will prove very entertaining to me. As to your letter the notice will tell you that I can-not comply with your request by sending the original manuscript. My first thought was to send it on receipt of your first letter; but fearing you might be delayed in completing your materials for the biography, and knowing the uncertainties of life, and not wishing to lose the man-uscript I concluded to send a copy. But I now regret I did not send the original. It would have been more satisfactory to you, and, with the accumulated materials in your hands, you, possibly, might have accounted for missing words and dates in the manuscript, and to have harmonized various parts better than I was able to do without facts which were not in my possession.

As to your fears that, in some instances, my grandfather made mis-takes in dates and names, I will say it is not at all improbable. The memory, whatever the age, is treacherous, and especially so is the memory of the aged as to names, dates and chronological order. And whilst my grandfather was noted for great memory and was possessed of a wonderful fund of miscellaneous knowledge, still his memory is not to be cited as an exception to the rule. In addition to the errors of memory there must be added, also, errors in believing "hear-says" and repeating them as facts without intention of misleading the reader. So far, then, as names, dates, chronological order and "hear-says" form a part of my grandfather's narrative, he may have made mistakes but aside from all of these there are the events to which they relate. The memory of even the aged, never loses its grip upon events if they are remarkable and impressive; as were the events narrated by my grandfather. And that they actually occurred I have not the shadow of a doubt; knowing the sterling integrity of the man as I did.

My grandfather evidently made one mistake in his narrative, as to a boy. When Boone and wife and the boy made the last visit to my grandfather, where the boy ate his birthday dinner, the boy is introduced as "Nathan, a nephew of Boones." And once afterwards he is called "nephew." But in other places, he is associated with Boone and wife as their "Son Nathan." Here I was puzzled. In the paragraph where the children of Daniel were enumerated I easily recognized Nathan as Daniel's son, but finding in the paragraph relating to the visit—Nathan, a son, and Nathan, a nephew, I was at a loss to determine what to do with it; it being evident there was present but one boy. And the most satisfactory solution to me was that he had associated in his mind a son and a nephew of Boone's, both named Nathan, with whom he associated more than a half century previous, and that under an undiscriminating lull of the memory, caused by writing the previous pages, he used son and nephew interchangeably without intending it. And as the preponderance seemed to be in favor of son I so wrote it and changed the phraseology in the contents to correspond. But even now it is a question whether the boy was a son or a nephew of Daniel Boone's. Still the difficulty raised no doubt in my mind as to whether a boy did or not eat his birthday dinner on the occasion referred to.

As to your saying that Boone's last return from North Carolina was in 1779 and that he remained at Boonesborough but a short time after his arrival before going on and locating in Athens, I would say that 1780, as inserted by me where the date was illegible, corresponds with the date subsequently given in the narrative, and was justified by Abbott's biography of Boone.

But in any case whether the date is right or wrong it remains true, doubtless, that the parties came together from North Carolina and that the journey was distinguished by the occurrences narrated by my grandfather.

Again thanking you for the books, and, hope that the copy sent you may, in some parts at least, be made available for your purpose of giving to the world an interesting and authentic biography of Daniel Boone. I am very truly yours,

F. W. Houston

P.S. Please excuse my use of this paper. It was all I could find out about the house when I sat down to write this letter.

F. W. H.

P.S. I intended to say, in the proper place, that, even, admitting the fact that Boone remained but a short time at Boonesborough before locating in Athens, this fact would not conflict with the narrative. Athens is but six or seven miles from Boonesborough, and is nearer Houston's Fort than Boonesborough is. So that Boone could have as conveniently done all that my grandfather gives him credit for, whether stationed in the one place or in the other.

F. W. H.

G

Included on DM 20C:89(1) is an old newspaper clipping—date and source unknown—of F. W. Houston's notice reporting the theft of his manuscripts.

Notice.—I either lost between North Middletown and Paris, or had taken from my buggy in the yard of Joseph Rion, in Paris, on the night of the 3d inst, the following documents: "A Sketch of the life and character of Daniel Boone," by Peter Houston, my grandfather; "an essay on moral philosophy," by Samuel Houston my father, and "Strictures of Infidelity," by John Q.A. Houston, my brother, for the recovery of which I will pay ten dollars. These documents were in manuscript written long since, and were highly prized by me as "keep sakes." They were on their way to Cincinnati to be bound in a volume.

F. W. H.

H

Last letter from F. W. Houston to Dr. Draper, DM 20C:91-92.

North Middletown, Ky
January 6, 1888

Lyman C. Draper
Madison, Wisconsin
Dear Sir:

Your letter of the 19th December was duly received—I have been confined to my room and have had no opportunity to see Mr. Scott except a few minutes. He promised me then to reflect and try to recall what information he could of reminisces . . . by his father as to his grandfather's sojourn at the Falls. I shall see him again within a few days and give you the result. I herewith send you the announcement of my grandfather's death which will show you that he was born 13 Dec. 1764. I had his full obituary notice but lost it when my residence was burned. He was never enrolled as a soldier, was not on the list of pensioners. His father—as I learned from him and from the autobiography written by him; was engaged in most of the pioneer battles in his state was in two battles in South Carolina—in which the colonies were defeated by the British, was in Pennsylvania among the troops under Patrick Henry and Campbell when they . . . . He was with the victorious pioneers who met and defeated the British at King's Mountain after my grandfather left for Kentucky. He was chief in providing subsistence for the volunteers at all points in the state where they were assembled or on the march. And all was conveyed on pack horses, and it was to assist him in this service that my grandfather was employed.

Hoping that I may get some information from Mr. Scott that will aid you in your biographical labors I am
Very Truly Yours,

F. W. Houston

P.S. I have again written to my relatives as to the autobiography, though I fear the document is lost, as a thorough search and inquiry was made for it upon my former application.

F. W. H.

I

In his final letter, F. W. Houston enclosed this undated, uncited copy of Peter Houston's obituary, DM 20C:92.

Departed from this life at the residence of . . . Alford, in Monroe County, Ind. on the 28th of Feb. 1855, Peter Houston, aged 90 years, two months, and 15 days. The deceased was one of the number, who united with Barton W. Stone on the Bible alone, at old Kane Ridge, at the time of the "great revival." And up to the day of his death he lived a very devoted Christian life. He loved the cause, and the brethren, and devoted much time to the study of the prophecies. And perhaps no man ever manifested more contempt for worldly honor, and fame, than he. But like a ripe shock of corn, he has been gathered to his fathers. M.

J

Theodore O'Hara (1820–1867), a native Kentuckian who fought in the Mexican War, joined Narcisco Lopez's expedition to Cuba in 1849, and served as lieutenant colonel of the Alabama 12th Infantry in the Civil War. He was Kentucky's first poet of note. Portions of his best-known poem, "The Bivouac of the Dead," are inscribed on the gates at the entry of Arlington National Cemetery. At an unknown date O'Hara penned this piece, "The Old Pioneer, Daniel Boone." In 1887, when F. W. Houston sent Dr. Draper Peter Houston's narrative, "A Sketch of the Life and Character of Daniel Boone," he enclosed a copy of Theodore O'Hara's Boone dirge. It is included here as a poignant close to the story of Houston's memoir and as an authentic but little seen literary piece of Kentuckiana and Boone folklore.

The Old Pioneer, Daniel Boone

A dirge for the brave old pioneer!
    Knight-errant of the wood!
Calmly beneath the green sod here,
    He rests from field and flood;
The war-whoop and the panther's screams
    No more his soul shall rouse,
For well the aged hunter dreams
    Beside his good old spouse.

A dirge for the brave old pioneer!
    Hushed now his rifle's peal—
The dews of many a vanish'd year
    Are on his rusted steel;
His horn and pouch lie mouldering
    Upon the cabin door—
The elk rests by the salted spring,
    Nor flees the fierce wild boar.

A dirge for the brave old pioneer!
    Old druid of the West!
His offering was the fleet wild deer;
    His shrine the mountain's crest.

Within his wildwood temple's space
    An empire's towers nod,
Where erst, alone of all his race,
    He knelt to nature's God.

A dirge for the brave old pioneer!
    Columbus of the land!
Who guided freedom's proud career
    Beyond the conquered strand;
And gave her pilgrims sons a home
    No monarch's step profanes,
Free as the chainless winds that roam
    Upon its boundless plains.

A dirge for the brave old pioneer!
    A dirge for his old spouse!
For her who blest his forest cheer,
    And kept his birchen house.
Now soundly by her chieftain may
    The brave old dame sleep on,
The red man's step is far away,
    The wolf's dread howl is gone.

A dirge for the brave old pioneer!
    His pilgrimage is done;
He hunts no more the grizzly bear,
    About the setting sun.
Weary at last of chase and life
    He laid him here to rest,
Nor recks he now what sport or strife
    Would tempt him further West.

A dirge for the brave old pioneer!
    The patriarch of his tribe!
He sleeps, no pompous pile marks where,
    No lines his deeds describe;
They raised no stone above him here,
    Nor carved his deathless name—
An empire is his sepulcher,
    His epitaph is Fame.

F. W. Houston (1818–1903), c. 1840s, at about the age he asked Peter Houston to write his remembrances of Daniel Boone. (GLADYS SANTEN)

Fannie Laurene Houston, c. 1840s, the wife of F. W. Houston. The couple raised eight children. (GLADYS SANTEN)

F. W. Houston in 1903, age eighty-five, with his great-grandson, Rene Houston Clark. One week after this picture was made, F. W. suffered a stroke and fell off this porch and died. (GLADYS SANTEN)

Hopewell Spring, or "The Big Spring." Here in 1780, James and Peter Houston built Fort Houston to protect them as they hunted and tanned hides. Houston Creek is about twenty yards away. The bridge is U.S. 68, once a buffalo path, now a state road.

The Attack by Indians on the Boones and John Stewart *is an engraving by an unknown hand—correctly depicting Long Hunters, Woodland Indians, a canebrake—and first appeared in 1812 as the frontispiece in Humphrey Marshall's* The History of Kentucky. *It is thought to be the first representation of Boone and his fellow hunters in Kentucky.*

Shawnee warrier, circa 1790s, drawn by Joseph Wabun. Draped over the warrior's shoulder is a white duffel blanket with blue stripe; tied around his red stroud leggings are finger-woven garters of red and blue wool; a blue cloth laps over his blue stroud breech-cloth; blue trade beads encircle his neck; his slit ear rims are distended; and his hair is roached.

A remnant of the buffalo path the Kentuckians followed on August 19, 1792, just minutes before the bloody ambush at the Battle of Blue Licks. (PHOTO BY DAVID E. SMITH)

This stone marks the mass grave of forty-three Americans killed during the Battle of Blue Licks. The British-allied Indians killed seventy-seven Kentuckians during the fifteen-minute fight. Many bodies were never recovered. (PHOTO BY DAVID E. SMITH)

On August 19, 1928, Kentuckians unveiled this obelisk erected near the mass grave on the Blue Licks battlefield in memory of the men slain at the site. (PHOTO BY DAVID E. SMITH)

Names of the survivors and the fallen are chiseled in the Blue Licks monument, as are these words by Daniel Boone: "So valiantly did our small party fight, that, to the memory of those who unfortunately fell in the battle, enough of honor cannot be paid." (PHOTO BY LAVINA TURBEVILLE BELUE)

Boone's last Kentucky cabin, built in 1795 at Brushy Creek, Nicholas County. Boone lived here until 1799, when he moved to Missouri. The cabin is about fourteen feet wide and eighteen feet long. It sits, rotting and ignored by the Commonwealth, on private land near a historical marker on U.S. Route 68. (PHOTO BY DAVID E. SMITH)

Col. Daniel Boon. In June 1820 Chester Harding painted a bust of Boone from life, and made two copies. Two weeks after Boone's death on September 26, Harding collaborated with engraver James O. Lewis to release this stipple engraving. (ORIGINAL ENGRAVING HOUSED AT THE MISSOURI HISTORICAL SOCIETY. REPRODUCTION BY PATHFINDER PRESS)

The grave of Daniel and Rebecca Boone. In 1845 a Kentucky delegation traveled to Tuque Creek, Missouri, to exhume the Boones' remains and inter them in the Frankfort Cemetery. In 1862 the state erected this fifteen-foot obelisk to their memory. In 1910 cemetery officials restored the pillar's bas-relief side panels and erected this fence after Union Civil War soldiers and vandals defaced the monument. (PHOTO BY DAVID E. SMITH)

One of the bas-relief panels of the Boone grave marker, symbolizing Boone as an heroic Indian fighter, an image that in life he never relished. (PHOTO BY DAVID E. SMITH)

Abbreviations

AR: *The American Revolution, 1775-1783: An Encyclopedia.* Edited by Dr. Richard L. Blanco. New York: Garland Publishing, 1993.

DM: Draper Manuscripts, State Historical Society of Wisconsin, Madison.

FCHQ: *Filson Club History Quarterly*

FWH: Franklin Warren Houston

JMF: John Mack Faragher. *Daniel Boone: The Life and Legend of an American Pioneer.* New York: Henry B. Holt, 1992.

KY: *The Kentucky Encyclopedia.* Edited by John E. Kleber. Lexington: University Press of Kentucky, 1992.

LCD: Lyman Copeland Draper

LIFE: "Life of Boone," incomplete manuscript by Lyman Copeland Draper

NB: Nathan Boone, interview with Lyman Copeland Draper, 1851

NOH: Neal Owen Hammon

PH: Peter Houston

RKHS: *Register of the Kentucky Historical Society.*

TFB: Ted Franklin Belue

Endnotes

INTRODUCTION

1. PH to FWH, May 2, 1842, DM 20C:84.
2. Information in the introduction regarding Houston genealogy and family history was largely derived from copies of two unpublished documents, "Lineage of Houston Family," by FWH, July 4, 1895; and "F. W. Houston's Letter to His Family Concerning Their Reunions," by FWH, c. 1890. The documents were generously provided by Mrs. Gladys Santen, of Paris, Kentucky, the great-great-great-granddaughter of Peter Houston.
3. The Great Revival, sometimes called the Second Great Awakening, swept across the American South beginning in 1800 and lasted until 1805. On August 8, 1801, at Cane Ridge, in east-central Bourbon County, Kentucky, near the site of Houston's Station, crowds up to twenty thousand came to hear as many as seven preachers preach simultaneously from stump pulpits. Cane Ridge minister Barton W. Stone lauded the Cane Ridge Revival for establishing clear doctrinal precepts but decried its fanatical emotionalism. Evangelical movements following the Cane Ridge Revival helped spawn the Christian Church (Disciples of Christ), the Christian Church, and the churches of Christ.
4. Discrepancies abound concerning Peter Houston's birth date. F. W. Houston–the family historian and a generally reliable source–noted that his grandfather was born April 2, 1761, a date which does not harmonize with his obituary notice. FWH to LCD, January 6, 1888, DM 20C:92.
5. FWH to LCD, November 14, 1887, DM 20C:83–84.
6. See LCD, *King's Mountain and its Heroes*, 2nd ed. (Baltimore: Baltimore Genealogical Publishing Company, 1969).
7. FWH to LCD, December 12, 1887, DM 20C:89.
8. FWH to LCD, November 2, 1889, DM 20C:88; see John S. C. Abbott, *Daniel Boone: Pioneer of Kentucky* (New York: Dodd and Mead, 1872).
9. See Abbott, *Pioneer*, 231, 237, 239.

HOUSTON'S NARRATIVE

1. Squire Boone, Sr., his wife, Sarah Morgan, and their children left Exeter, Pennsylvania, for the five-hundred-mile trek to North Carolina in the late spring of 1750. Daniel, their sixth child, born on October 22, 1734, was nearing his sixteenth year. Other children of Squire, Sr., and Sarah Boone were Sarah, b. June 7, 1724; Israel, b. May 9, 1726; Samuel, b. May 20, 1728; Jonathan, b. December 6, 1730; Elizabeth, b. February 5, 1732; Mary, b. November 3, 1736; George, b. January 2, 1739; Edward, b. November 19, 1740; Squire, b. October 5, 1744, and Hannah,

b. August 1746. Several other family members and friends also joined the Boone party. See LIFE, DM 1B:36–37; for the most extensive compilation of Boone genealogy to date, see Hazel Atterbury Spraker, *The Boone Family* (Baltimore: Genealogical Publishing Company, 1974), 36–40.

2. The narrative erroneously cites this date as "June the 4th 1756." See DM 20C:84(10).

3. John Findley was licensed as a trader from 1744 to 1746. George Croghan, an Indian trader and entrepreneur, hired Findley in the 1750s. Findley may have once been employed by the Philadelphia-based firm of Baynton, Wharton and Morgan. See Charles A. Hanna to Reuben Gold Thwaites, March 22, 1902, LIFE, DM 2B:173–74; see also LIFE, DM 2B:162–73; Charles A. Hanna, *The Wilderness Trail* (New York: Knickerbocker Press, 1911), 2:2, 38, 155–56, 212–40.

4. Boone and John Findley's companions in May 1769, the date of Boone's first foray into the Kentucky Bluegrass, were John Stuart (Boone's brother-in-law), Joseph Holden, James Mooney, and William Cooley. Squire Boone, Jr. (Daniel's brother), joined the hunters after the fall harvest. Peter Houston's reference to a "William Sconce" is most likely meant to be Alexander Neely. After John Stuart's disappearance and death at the hands of Indians, Neely left Boone's party to return to the settlements. Indians killed Neely and his son James in Kentucky in 1796. LIFE, 2B:173–74; for Neely see LIFE, DM 3B:65–67; also JMF, 82–84.

5. An error. When the Shawnee captured Boone, his companions escaped and later rejoined him. Mooney, Cooley, Holden, and Findley returned east. Findley returned to the life of an Indian trader, but Seneca warriors robbed him of five hundred pounds worth of trade goods. Once wounded by gunshot, by 1772 he had vanished from history. In 1774, Indians killed Mooney at the Battle of Point Pleasant.

6. An error. See previous note. Upon leaving Kentucky in 1771, just past the Cumberland Gap, Cherokee warriors confiscated Boone's peltry and accoutrements. In May 1771, Boone returned to the Yadkin Valley poorer than he was when he had left for Kentucky two years previously.

7. The narrative cites this date as "the 15th of September 1771." See DM 20C:84(3).

8. During the summer of 1773, Boone left the upper Yadkin Valley for Castle's Woods settlement in southeastern Virginia on the Clinch River. On September 25, 1773, Boone and his party of forty to fifty friends and family left Castle's Woods for Kentucky. See JMF, 91–92.

9. An error. See previous note.

10. Not true. One of Boone's men discovered the massacre and relayed the news to the main party camped three miles ahead.

11. No other account of this episode lists James L. Brown. A war party of Shawnee and Cherokee tortured and killed James Boone (Daniel and Rebecca's firstborn son, age sixteen), John and Richard Mendinall, Henry Russell, a youth named Drake, and a slave, Charles. Isaac Crabtree, severely wounded in the ambush, survived. See LOB, DM 3B:96–98; JMF, 92–94, Spraker, *Boone*, 65.

12. Marginal note by LCD, DM 20C:84(4). "Did not return to North Carolina."

13. The narrative erroneously notes that Boone's migration to Kentucky was that autumn. But Boone and his team of thirty woodsmen began their trek to blaze the Wilderness Road on March 13, 1775, arriving at the site of what would become Boonesborough on April 1. See note 19.

14. By 1774, unclaimed land in Kentucky was offered to Virginia veterans of the French and Indian War (1755–63) in the following allotments for each tour of duty: an ensign was entitled to one thousand acres, a sergeant two hundred acres, and a private fifty acres. In 1773, Captain Thomas Bullitt led the first expedition

of forty surveyors from Fincastle County, Virginia, to Kentucky. Other Fincastle County survey teams reached the Falls of the Ohio by May 1774. Before fleeing Kentucky because of raids that led to Lord Dunmore's War, the surveyors had claimed 153,000 acres. James Harrod, John Floyd, James Douglas, Isaac Hite, and Hancock Taylor acted as deputy surveyors. Boone and Michael (Holsteiner) Stoner left the Clinch on June 26, found the surveyors, warned them of hostilities, and guided a few of the men home. For more on the complexity of presettlement Kentucky land dealings, the surveyors, and Boone and Stoner's role in the matter, see NOH, *Early Kentucky Land Records: 1773–1780* (Louisville, KY: Filson Club Publications, 1992), xii–xvii; see also NOH, "The Fincastle Surveyors at the Falls of the Ohio: 1774," *FCHQ* 47(1973): 14–28. See also NOH, "Fincastle Surveyors in the Bluegrass: 1774," *RKHS* 70(1972): 277–94.

15. The "one man" referred to may be Hancock Taylor or one of his comrades. Taylor was one of the Fincastle surveyors who came to Kentucky in the spring of 1774 with Colonel William Preston. Taylor, James Strother, and Abraham Heponstall were paddling across the Kentucky in a bark canoe on July 27 when Shawnee marksmen fired on them, killing Strother and wounding Taylor, who died days later. On July 8, about twenty Shawnee ambushed John Knox's party near Harrod's Town, killing James Cowan and James Hamilton. The rest of the surveyors camped at Harrod's Town, where Boone and Stoner found them, as Boone reported, "well drove in by Indians." See NOH, *Early Kentucky Land Records: 1773–80*, Filson Club Publication, 2nd ser., no. 5 (Louisville, KY: Butler Book Company, 1992), xi–xiv, 17–18, 42–44; for a listing of the surveyors, see NOH, "Pioneers in Kentucky, 1773–1775," *FCHQ* 55(1981): 270–71.

16. On January 6, 1775, the North Carolina lawyer Richard Henderson, Thomas and Nathaniel Hart, William Johnston, John Luttrell, and others formally organized the Transylvania Land Company. On March 17, 1775, at Sycamore Shoals, Tennessee, the Cherokee, for ten thousand pounds in sterling and trade goods, sold the company their claim to Kentucky and Tennessee—roughly seventeen to twenty million acres—between the Kentucky and Cumberland Rivers. Attending the Watauga Treaty were, among others, James Robertson, John Sevier, Isaac Shelby, the Bledsoe brothers, Richard Callaway, Nathaniel Henderson, and William Cocke. For a dated but thorough explanation of Henderson's illegal act and of the duplicity practiced by both sides in the land grab, see William Stewart Lester, *The Transylvania Company* (Spencer, IN: Samuel R. Guard and Company), 1–47; for personnel, see LIFE, DM 3B:171.

17. For his services in blazing the Wilderness Road, Boone received from the Transylvania Company two thousand acres, which he forfeited without compensation when Virginia voided Henderson's Kentucky claims in 1778.

18. The Treaty of Sycamore Shoals may have been a case of mutual fraud. It is doubtful that the Cherokee held title to all the land they sold, and the illegal Transylvania Company was negotiating without the consent of the Crown. In addition, the territory was protected by the Proclamation of 1763, the Treaty of Fort Stanwix (1768), and Virginia law. Tribal leaders may have viewed the treaty as expedient—the politics of Indian survival under Anglo pressure. Kentucky historian Neal O. Hammon says of Boone's role during the Watauga Treaty: "Actually, there is some doubt that Boone was ever present during this treaty, which was signed on 17 March 1775. Boone and his road cutters gathered at Long Island on the Holston, about thirty miles away, and left for Kentucky on 13 March." Regarding the complexities of the Sycamore Shoals Treaty, see Tom Hatley, *The Dividing Paths: Cherokees and South Carolinians through the Revolutionary Era* (New York: Oxford University Press, 1995), 217–21; Colin G. Calloway, *The American Revolution in Indian Country: Crisis and Diversity in Native American Communities* (New York:

Cambridge University Press, 1995), 189–90; for the history of the Transylvania Company, the March 1775 conference, the treaty, and the personnel, see Lester, *Transylvania*, 1–47; for Boone's role, see NOH, "Pioneer Kentucky History: Separating the Facts from the Myths," n.p.; also see statements by Daniel Bryan, Nathaniel Hart, and Nathan Boone, LIFE, DM 3B:188(1).

19. Boone's party of about thirty woodcutters left the Holston on March 13, 1775, and arrived at what would become the site of Boonesborough on April 1. Besides Boone, the party of woodsmen included Squire Boone, Benjamin Cutbirth, Michael Stoner, Colonel Richard Callaway, William Hays, David Gass, William Bush, Edmund Jennings, John Kennedy, John Vardeman, James Nall, William Moore, William Miller, Reuben and Bartlett Searcy, Samuel Tate, John King, Oswell Towns, Capt. William Twetty and his slave, Samuel Coburn, James Bridges, Thomas Johnson, John Hart, William Hicks, James Peeke, and Felix Walker. Susannah Hays (wife of William Hays and Boone's oldest daughter) and Callaway's African slave woman cooked and tended camp. LIFE, DM 3B:173–74.

20. On June 13, 1775, Boone left Kentucky to return to North Carolina with the rest of his family. While back at the Yadkin, Rebecca gave birth to a baby boy, William, who died a few days later. Boone and his kin were back at Boonesborough by September 8. See JMF, 126–27.

21. An overstatement. Boone once remarked in his old age, "the world had taken great liberties . . . it is true that I have suffered many hardships and miraculously escaped many perils, but others of my companions have experienced the same." Simon Kenton, James Harrod, George Rogers Clark, Christopher Gist, Casper Mansker, John Floyd, Spencer and Laban Records, Hugh F. Bell, Hancock Taylor, Bland Ballard, and many other pioneers and their wives endured privation, capture, wounds, loss of loved ones, and came near death. Boone, who loathed putting himself forward, willingly left the limelight to his peers.

22. The entire episode of Boone's capture and life among the Shawnee is best covered in LOB, 4B:145–201; for a more accessible rendering, see JMF, 160–76; for an expansive overview on the fate of Boone's men after their capture on the Lower Blue Licks in February 1778, see TFB, "Terror in the Canelands: The Fate of Daniel Boone's Saltboilers," *FCHQ* 68(1994): 3–34.

23. Boone's dangerous foray against the Shawnee is known as the Paint Lick episode. Daniel Trabue heard Boone testify in his own defense at his court-martial the fall of 1778. He wrote that Boone said he knew where thirty to forty warriors were camped on a branch of the Scioto River, "and if a few men would go with him he would conduct them to this little Camp, and as these indians was rich in good horses and beaver fur they could go and make a great speck." Boone and his scouts disguised themselves in Indian garb, daubed their faces with war paint, and after crossing the Ohio on rafts, they stole three horses and plunder, wounded two warriors, and took one scalp. With Boone was Simon Kenton, Alexander Montgomery, John Holder, Pemberton Rollins, Jesse Hodges, and about fourteen others. See Chester Raymond Young, ed., *Westward into Kentucky: The Memoirs of Daniel Trabue* (Lexington: University Press of Kentucky), 57. Trabue's narrative, along with notes, annotation, and relevant correspondence by LCD, is originally found in DM 57J; see also LIFE, DM 4B:206–8.

24. In the narrative, the date is cited as "the 8th of August." This error may be attributed to F. W. Houston's transcription, who copied the wrong date from Abbott, *Boone*, 207, who had in turn copied the erroneous date from Filson. See John Filson, *The Discovery, Settlement and Present State of Kentucke* (New York: Corinth Books, 1962) 67–68. Filson's *Kentucke* was originally published in 1784.

25. An oft-repeated error. There was no "Duquesne" at the siege of Boonesborough. Captain Isadore Dechaine, interpreter for the Wyandot and Ottawa, Peter Druil-

lard, a British Indian trader, and an African ex-slave named Pompey (whom the Shawnee purportedly kidnapped as a boy in Virginia during the French and Indian War), were present. Houston's reference to "General Hamilton" is to Lieutenant-Governor Henry Hamilton, then commander of Fort Detroit. See LIFE, 4B:210–11. For Pompey's role during the Boonesborough siege and the conflicting accounts of his death, see TFB, "Did Daniel Boone Kill Pompey, the Black Shawnee, at the 1778 Siege of Boonesborough?" *FCHQ* 67 (1993): 5–22; regarding African-Americans in the western theater of the Revolutionary War, see TFB, "Blacks on the Western Frontier," *AR*, 1:128–29.

26. Estimates of the number of Indians that attacked Boonesborough vary. Boone, prone to understatement, said there were about 440 Ohio Valley Indians present, plus forty French-Canadians, and British rangers. Fort defenders numbered about sixty men, women, children, and slaves and their families. See LIFE, DM 4B:211. Regarding the two-day parley and the skirmish that precipitated the nine-day siege, see LIFE, DM 4B:211–30.

27. In DM 20C:84(4), the narrative erroneously names Squire Boone, Jr., as "Jonathan." During the fray that erupted at the treaty negotiations, Indians shot Squire Boone in the shoulder and struck Daniel a glancing tomahawk blow to the head. LIFE, DM 4B:227.

28. Draper's account of the siege is found in LIFE, DM 4B:227–50; American casualties include two dead—London, a slave owned by Richard Henderson, and David Bundrin—and four wounded—Daniel Boone, Squire Boone, Jr., Jemima Boone Callaway, and Pemberton Rollins. Daniel Boone recorded thirty-seven Indians killed "and a great number wounded." LIFE, DM 4B:251.

29. The narrative omits the most humiliating ordeal Boone ever endured, an attempt by Col. Richard Callaway and others to court-martial him. The trial was held at Logan's Station in the fall of 1778. Callaway asserted that in February 1778 when the Shawnee captured Boone, to save himself, Boone led them to his men camped on the Lower Blue Licks to surrender them as prisoners of war. And while a captive at Detroit, Callaway insisted, Boone struck a deal with Lieutenant-Governor Henry Hamilton to "give up all the people of Boonesborough . . . [to] live under British jurisdiction." Callaway averred that on August 30, 1778, when Boone raided the Shawnee camped at Paint Creek, his rash act weakened Boonesborough's defenses and brought the Shawnee upon them. And, Callaway charged, during the two-day negotiations before the siege, Boone's willingness to parley with the Shawnee beyond range of the fort put Boonesborough's officers in danger. Callaway concluded, wrote Daniel Trabue, the only eyewitness of the trial to leave a record of it, that "Boon was in favuor of the britesh government, that all his conduct proved it." But Boone vigorously defended himself.

Capt. Daniel Boon sayed the reason he give up these men at the blue licks was that the Indeans told him they was going to Boonsborough to take the fort. Boon said he thought he would use some stratigem. He thought the fort was in bad order and the Indeans would take it easy. He (Boon) said he told the Indians the fort was very strong and too many men for them, that he was friendly to them (and the officers at Detroyt) and he would go and shew them some men—to wit, 26—and he would go with them to Detroyt and these men also, and when they come to take Boonsbourough they must have more warriers than they now had. Boon said he told them all these tails to fool them. He also said he Did tell the Britesh officers he would be friendly to them and try to give up Boons-bourough but that he was a trying to fool them.

The jury found him not guilty and promoted him to major of the militia. Settlers debated the issue for years, but Boone remained forever silent about the episode. See Trabue, *Kentucky*, 63–64.

30. A chronological error. Boone returned to Kentucky from the Yadkin in October 1779. In February 1780, he and a companion left Virginia, and during a night's stay at an inn, thieves robbed Boone of $20,000 in deflated Revolutionary War currency entrusted to him by Kentuckians purchasing land claims to be filed at Williamsburg. Boone discovered a small amount of the cash hidden in bottles in the inn's cellar, but he never recovered the entire sum. Boone, having locked his door at the inn from the inside, believed that the landlord drugged him and crept in during the night, or that an old woman acting as an accomplice had hidden in the room as he slept and absconded with the money. Boone sold much of his land to pay off the debt, but it took years to clear his name. "It was," recalled Nathan Boone, "a great loss." NB to LCD, DM 6S:145–46; see JMF, 208–9.

31. Boone and his family left the Yadkin in September 1779 and were back in Kentucky by that October. By Christmas he left Boonesborough to start Boone's Station (near present-day Athens).

32. An error. At the time of this 1779 migration, Daniel and Rebecca Boone had seven living children. Of those seven, Susannah and Jemima were married and living at Boonesborough with their husbands, William Hays and Flanders Callaway. But the other five Boone children, Israel, Levina, Rebecca, Daniel Morgan, and Jesse, traveled with the caravan. For more information on the children of Daniel and Rebecca Boone, see note 71.

33. Boone's return party to Kentucky in the fall of 1779 numbered about one hundred.

34. Olive Boone, wife of Nathan, told Draper how frontier women made sieves. Settlers bent a strip of green hickory bark round, lapped and tied the ends with a leather thong, then stitched a damp deerhide—after first soaking the skin in a caustic bath of wood ashes to remove the hair—over the hoop to dry as taut as a drum head, then poked holes in the skin with a hot wire. See Olive Boone to LCD, 1851, DM 6S:243.

35. Jemima Boone's (1762–1829) affinity for water was a bit of a family joke, resulting in her nickname of "Duck." On July 14, 1776, Indians captured Jemima and Fanny and Betsy Callaway canoeing on the Kentucky about one hundred yards from Boonesborough. Daniel Boone and a band of Kentuckians rescued them three days later. In 1777, Jemima married Flanders Callaway and in 1799 she and her husband moved to Missouri with her father. For a biographical sketch of Jemima Boone Callaway, see Spraker, *Family*, 119–21.

36. Quoted in DM 20C:84(15).

37. "Johnny cake" is a corruption of "journey cake." Journey cakes were made of cornmeal and water and cooked on a flat rock placed in coals. Or, to make "ash cakes," the ashes would be blown off the coals and the cornmeal mix glopped on the cinders to cook. Slaves in the South baked cornmeal batter on hoe blades over fires, hence the term "hoe cakes." When baked in a Dutch oven or skillet with a heated lid, settlers referred to journey cakes as "pones" or "loafs," and called pones baked in large batches "dodgers." Mush—boiled cornmeal mixed with milk, honey, or butter—was a frontier staple and a favorite of Boone's, who in his old age had mush served to him in his prized china bowl.

38. Squire Boone, Jr. (1744–1815), married Jane Van Cleve on August 8, 1765, and had five children: Jonathan (b. August 30, 1766); Moses (b. February 23, 1769); Isaiah (b. March 13, 1772); Sarah (b. September 26, 1774); and Enoch (b. October 16, 1777). For an accurate biographical sketch of Squire Boone, Jr., see Spraker, *Family*, 72–83.

39. In F. W. Houston's transcription, he erroneously inserts the name Israel, who was Boone's son killed at the Battle of Blue Licks on August 19, 1782.

40. Regarding the death of Edward "Ned" Boone, see Nancy O'Malley, *Stockading Up: A Study of Pioneer Stations in the Inner Bluegrass Region of Kentucky*, Archaeological Report 127 (Frankfort: Kentucky Heritage Council, 1987), 173–74; also Spraker, *Family*, 70–72; see also note 66.

41. Marginal note by LCD: "It was ten years earlier."

42. The role of salt in western expansion can hardly be overstated. In the East, people living in the backcountry made yearly pilgrimages to the coast—to Charleston, South Carolina; Boiling Point or Roanoke, Virginia; or Cape Fear, North Carolina—to trade for salt. Salt springs near the Great Kanawha (New River), Holston, and Cumberland Rivers and in Ohio, Tennessee, and Kentucky were key factors in allowing settlers to cross the Appalachians knowing they could feed themselves. At the Lower Blue Licks, it took 840 gallons of water to make one bushel of salt. See Thomas D. Clark, "Salt: a Factor in the Settlement of Kentucky," *FCHQ* 12(1938): 42–52; see also Frederick Jackson Turner, *The Frontier in American History*, 3rd ed. (Malabar, FL: Robert E. Krieger, 1985), 17–18; regarding the saline effluence at the Lower Blue Lick, see LIFE, DM 4B:146.

43. Making fire with flint and steel is easy and quick. One strikes a flint shard against a tempered steel striker, directing the sparks to a small square of charred cotton or linen. Hunters used charred natural substances, like pithy wood and fungus, referred to as "char," "punk-wood," "spunk," or "touch-wood," in place of burnt cloth. A pinch of gunpowder, if it could be spared, might be used too. Once a spark catches on the char, the glowing cloth is placed in a nest of finely shredded tinder of cedar bark or tow and blown into a flame.

44. Peter and James Houston built Fort Houston on Houston Creek, about one hundred yards northeast of the present site of the Paris courthouse in Bourbon County, and lived there for about three years. According to Kentucky archaeologist Nancy O'Malley, the Houston brothers "apparently never held title to their station location." The small outpost was a well-known stopping place for settlers, salt boilers, and hunters. Archaeologists have not determined its exact site, but a stone marker marks its approximate location. For a brief biographical sketch of Peter and James Houston, and notes on their land dealings and on Houston's Station, see O'Malley, *Stations*, 66–68.

45. For frontier techniques of tanning hides and Anglo and Indian woodland attire, see TFB, "Indian-Influenced Woodsmen of the Cane," in *The Book of Buckskinning VII*, ed. William H. Scurlock (Texarkana, TX: Scurlock Publishing Company, 1995), 42–77.

46. West of the Appalachians, the winter of 1779–80, the Hard Winter, was the hardest winter settlers ever endured. Heavy snows were falling by early November and did not completely melt off until the following March. The Ohio and Cumberland froze over, stopping shipments of supplies such as corn, meat, and tallow from Fort Pitt. Animals froze to death, causing further food shortages and, in some cases, health hazards from eating putrid meat hacked from the rotting, half-frozen cow and horse carcasses that dotted pastures. During the Hard Winter, many settlers died from starvation, disease, or exposure.

47. By this date at the Falls of the Ohio, Indian attacks became frequent as atrocities by the Shawnee—called by Colonel John Floyd "those execrable Hell hounds"— worsened. Floyd, surveyor and leader of the Jefferson County militia, worked

hard to keep stations at the Falls and Beargrass Creek in meat. "Whole families are destroyed," he wrote on April 16, 1781, to George Rogers Clark. "Our dependence to support our families is upon getting wild meat and this is procured with great difficulty and danger." Many whites shot Indians on sight, while the Indians fought desperately to drive the white intruders from their lands. Material on John Floyd was taken from Hambleton Tapp, "Colonel John Floyd, Kentucky Pioneer," *FCHQ* 15(1941): 1–24; see also John Floyd Papers, transcribed by NOH, housed at the Filson Club, Louisville, Kentucky.

48. In 1779, Colonel John Floyd built the first settlement on the middle fork of Beargrass Creek, in Jefferson County, and named it Floyd's Station (sometimes called Beargrass Station). On April 9, 1783, along the westernmost terminus of the Wilderness Road, Indians shot Floyd, who died two days later. Squire Boone built his station in the spring of 1780 at a site called the Painted Stone in Shelby County, approximately twenty-five miles from the Beargrass settlements. See Vincent Akers, "The Low Dutch Company: A History of the Holland Dutch Settlements of the Kentucky Frontier," reprinted from The Holland Society of history *de Halve Maen*, 55(1980): 14.

49. Simon Girty (1741–1818) is one of the most controversial men of the Ohio Valley. He emerged in the early nineteenth century as the prototypical "white savage renegade," but much of the real man is hidden behind myths, distortions, and half-truths. Indians captured Simon at age fourteen along with his brothers, Thomas, George and James, and separated them. Thomas, the eldest, soon escaped and returned to Anglo life. The Seneca adopted Simon. The Delaware adopted and freed George. Like James, adopted by Shawnee, George kept his tribal identity till the end of his days. All three were active in the British Indian Department, but Simon's role as a "white Indian" was more complex than that of his brothers. Deeply imprinted by native life, yet unable to cut his ties to Anglo society, Simon Girty lived on the fringes of both, truly belonging to neither. Through eighteenth-century American eyes it is not hard to see why Simon Girty—Patriot-turned-Tory, defender of Indian rights, willing tool of the British Indian Department—had a price on his head. Yet Girty helped those he could. He befriended Boone during his Shawnee days, and was a sworn brother to Simon Kenton and saved Kenton's life. He also saved John Burkhart, Thomas Ridout, Samuel Murphy, William May, Margaret Handley Erskine, Henry Baker, and at least a dozen more captives. TFB, *Buckskinning VII*, 58–59; see Consul Wilshire Butterfield, *History of the Girtys*, 2nd ed. (Columbus, OH: Long's College Book Co., 1950); Colin C. Calloway, "Simon Girty: Interpreter and Intermediary," *Being and Becoming Indian: Biographical Studies of North American Frontiers*, ed. James A. Clifton (Prospect Heights, IL: Waveland Press, 1989), 38–58; Colin C. Calloway, "Neither White nor Red: White Renegades on the American Indian Frontier," *Western Historical Quarterly* 17, 1(1986): 43–66; Philip Hoffman, "Simon Girty," *AR*, 1:660–64.

50. Bryan's Station was two hundred yards long and fifty yards wide, with twelve-foot walls, corner blockhouses, and twenty cabins. Forty-four Americans defended Bryan's during the siege of August 15–17, 1782. Captains Alexander McKee and William Caldwell and British Indian agent Simon Girty led three hundred Wyandot, Chippewa, and Ottawa and fifty Rangers against Bryan's, killing two and wounding two. Indian losses are unknown. During the attack, the Indians stole horses, cut down corn, ignited fields, and slaughtered hogs, cattle, and sheep. On Monday, August 19, 1782, the Indians ambushed Kentuckians pursuing them at the Lower Blue Licks. See Richard H. Collins, "The Siege of Bryan's Station," *RKHS* 36(1938): 15–25; TFB, "Siege of Bryan's Station Kentucky: August 15–17, 1782," *AR*, 1:189–191; for diagrams of the fort, maps, and personnel, see O'Malley, *Stations*, 178–87.

51. American leaders at the Battle of Blue Licks were Colonel John Todd (1750–82), whose Fayette County forces guarded the center rank and to whom fell the duty of leadership; Colonel Stephen Trigg (1742–82), who commanded the right flank; and Colonel Daniel Boone (1734–1820), who led the left flank. Indians killed Todd and Trigg in the first blasts of the battle; they were buried in a mass grave at the site.

52. Indians made flaming arrows by affixing slivers of shagbark hickory or some other scaly bark to the base of the shaft next to the point, stuffing tow mixed with gunpowder in the bark, lighting it, then shooting the arrows in a high arc so as to stick them in the cedar shakes with which outposts were shingled. Attackers also tied small cotton or linen bags holding gunpowder near the flaming arrows' tips to ignite upon impact. Warriors made torches of rolled sheets of bark, "dry splints," or cane bundles wrapped with oily flax or rags to throw at the bases of forts or over palisades. For fire arrows and torches, see John Gass to LCD, April 1844, DM 24C:73(10–13); also Daniel Bryan to LCD, April 1844, DM 22C:10(9).

53. Hugh McGary is the most controversial Kentuckian at the Battle of Blue Licks and has taken his share of the blame as the hothead whose actions ignited the fiasco. But during deliberations the day before the fight, when both Boone and McGary had advised caution, one man there chided McGary and implied that he was a coward, which infuriated him. This may help explain McGary's outburst that triggered the Americans' headlong rush into the brilliant ambush set for them by McKee, Caldwell, Girty, and their Indian allies. For an intensely rendered account of the Battle of Blue Licks, see JMF, 216–25.

54. That McGary's insubordination was partly to blame for the massacre at Blue Licks cannot be doubted. Still, the rest of the men—frothing for a fight after the ruin caused to Bryan's Station two days before—eagerly followed McGary, as did the militia leaders, who should have stopped him.

55. According to Boone's nephew Daniel Bryan, at the Battle of Blue Licks Boone carried a long fowler—an unrifled, smooth-bore gun used for bird hunting or fowling, also known as a "smooth-rifle"—loaded with three to four undersized balls and seventeen to nineteen buckshot. Such a devastating charge was perfect for close-in bush fighting, a scenario Boone anticipated. See John Bakeless, *Daniel Boone: Master of the Wilderness*, 3rd ed. (Lincoln, NE: Bison, 1989), 298; NB to LCD, DM 65:154; see also NB, DM 65:154ff.

56. Estimates regarding Colonel Benjamin Logan's reinforcements number as high as five hundred men. See Nicky Hughes, "Battle of Blue Licks," *KY*, 92–93.

57. Indian casualties are unknown. Levi Todd, who was there, reported that "the enemy must have suffered considerably." Quoted in TFB, "Battle of Blue Licks," *AR*, 1:133–36.

58. Houston's report notwithstanding, the Indians took several whites captive to burn at their villages across the Ohio. Jesse Yocum, who escaped, declared that he "did not know how many they burned but the smell of a human was the awfullest smell he ever [smelled] in his life." Quoted in TFB, "Battle of Blue Licks," *AR*, 1:136; for an eyewitness account of death at the stake, see TFB, "Crawford's Sandusky Expedition: May–June 1782," *AR*, 1:416–20.

59. Americans lost 77 men out of a force of 182, equaling one-thirteenth of Kentucky's militia. With the frontier less defensible, many settlers fled east of the Blue Ridge. Kentuckians attending the site a week later buried more than forty corpses in a mass grave. To honor the Americans slain at Blue Licks—one of the last battles of the Revolution—the commonwealth dedicated a monument on the battlefield on August 19, 1928. In the obelisk are chiseled Daniel Boone's words: "So valiantly did our small party fight, that, to the memory of those who unfortunately fell in the battle, enough of honor cannot be paid."

60. In November 1782, George Rogers Clark and 1,050 frontiersmen launched a

devastating counterattack on the Indians, plundering, burning villages and crops, killing livestock. It was the Shawnee—a tribe marginally represented at the fights at Bryan's Station and Blue Licks—who bore the brunt of Clark's vengeance.

61. Ultimately Boone owned about thirty thousand acres of Kentucky land, most of which he sold to pay debts. For an overview of the Boone's Station legal dispute, which appeared on the court docket as *Boofman vs. Hickman*, see O'Malley, *Stations*, 175–78; see also JMF, 242–45.

62. The Spanish government granted Boone 1,000 arpents (850 acres) of land in the Femme Osage district of Missouri. Boone's tract was officially surveyed on January 9, 1800. See Oliver, *Descendants*, 10.

63. Michael Stoner (1748–1815) was a tough, stout man, full of fun, whose German accent was so thick that he called Captain Boone "Gabtain Schpoon." Stoner was a crack shot and one of Boone's most reliable companions, said to have hunted with the famous woodsman even as far as the Missouri River in 1810. See Mrs. William Breckenridge Ardery, *Historical Scrapbook: Bourbon County, Kentucky* (Paris, KY: privately published, 1939), 10–11.

64. This anecdote is found in DM 20C:84(45–47).

65. During their Pennsylvania years, Boone's parents were Quakers, or members of the Society of Friends. Before migrating to North Carolina in 1750, Squire Boone, Sr. was formally excommunicated from the Quakers because two of his children had married out of the faith. Throughout most of his life Daniel remained unchurched, but his letters reveal that he had a strong faith in God and in Providential care. In later years he frequently attended church services, was an avid Bible reader, believing strongly, he said, "in the great truths of Christianity," and had his children baptized. Peter Houston was a Presbyterian, but after Kentucky's Cane Ridge Revival in 1801 he joined those doctrinally allied with Barton W. Stone. See Introduction, note 2.

66. As mentioned in note 40, this portion of the narrative is chronologically out of order. For more on the death of Edward "Ned" Boone, see "Perticulars of E Boons Death," E. B. Scholl to LCD, January 5, 1856, DM 23C:104, as transcribed in O'Malley, *Stations*, 174, and noted as follows:

Daniel & Edward was hunting meete for the station and had with them 4 horses 2 they road and 2 they packed they had got as much as the 2 pack Horses would carry and camped in the neighborhood of the Blue Licks on the Licking River and started in to the Licks thinking to take the first game that came in the Lycks Just as the [they?] raised over the ridge in site of the Licks they saw fourteen Indians at the same time the indians saw them and appeared from their actions to have known who they was they turned there horses for Lexington and rode as fast as was thout advisale untill the after noon and came to a stream in Montgomery Co called Hinkston and Edward being a great favorite to horses proposed stoping and let there horses feed and rest Daniel replied that he thot the velians new them and would follow but Edward said he thout they had road fast anuf to put sufficient distance between them and give them time to rest and feed Daniel observed that about a mile from them there was a verry pretty grassy lick on the opposit side and they would ride into the stream and follow the same [to] the sd lick and stop when they got there they onladed there horses and turned them on the grass Daniel feeling oneasey sayed to Edward who had gathered some hickreynuts he had better keep a good lookout and he would take his gun and walk up the stream. here we must resort to the presumption as appears they was in site when the 2 brothers sepperated and had a greed amongst themselves for seven followed Daniel and the other seven crawled so near as to enable five of them to shoot Edward at the same time and the only thing that saved Daniel was he shot a bear and at the crack of his rifle the other seven fired at Edward an looking round he saw the seven that was dodging him so neare as to pere at him and made several ball holes threw his hunting shirt he knew what was the fate of his brother he ameediately run for the cain to screen him the indians set there dog on him and he tryed to coax the dog then to agravate him but to no purpose the constant baying of the dog gave the indians the advantage as he had to keep in the cane they could hear him by the bay of the dog at last he shot the dog and stopped so neare as to heare them consult and they said he would kill them all if they followed him he said if they concluded to follow him he would shoot and run in the cane and hide and shoot as they would be oblige to follow his tract and he could watch his bac track and shoot the whole of them he then start for Lexington whilst they was at breakfast the ameediately resed a company and when they got to the plase there was a wildcat siting at the wound in the breast for the indians had scalped and strup Edward then they buried him on the side of the hill I have been past the plase when a boy several times.

67. This note by F. W. Houston to Draper is written in the margin of DM 20C:84(50): "In 1842 when I received this sketch I went to James Bryan's (Cousin to Daniel's wife and to William Bryan, Boone's brother-in-law) and got him to take me to this buck-eye tree (he then owned the land) and I saw the letters, though dimmed by growth of the tree. They have since been ruined with the 'N' left off. 'Boone' alone was recut. The tree is still standing. I saw it a week ago."

68. That Boone moved to Limestone in 1783 is oft-quoted lore that may not be true, as the issue is muddied by two conflicting accounts that do not harmonize with known Boone chronology. In 1851, Nathan Boone told Lyman Draper that in 1783 his father moved about five miles west of Boone's Station to Marble Creek and lived there until 1785, then moved the family on to Limestone. But Boone's

nephew Daniel Bryan noted that after Boone "left Marble Creek he moved up on Sandy [River] or K[anawha], because he was so troubled by preemptions and etc." Compare NB to LCD, DM 6S:159, with Daniel Bryan to John D. Shane, c. 1843, DM 22C:14(14).

69. These prisoner exchanges were in Maysville, August 1787. During the lengthy parley, several Shawnee stayed at Boone's inn.

70. The accuracy of these dates cannot be determined. In 1789, Daniel and Rebecca moved to Point Pleasant, West Virginia. In 1792, they emigrated near to Charlestown, western Virginia. In 1795, they relocated to Brushy Fork, Boone's last Kentucky home before he left for Missouri in 1799. The old cabin still exists on private land near its original site off Highway 68 between Frankfort and Maysville.

71. An error. Nathan Boone, Daniel and Rebecca's last child, was born March 2, 1781, at Boone's Station, Fayette County, Kentucky, and died October 16, 1856, at Ash Grove, in Green County, Missouri. Daniel and Rebecca's other children were James Boone (May 3, 1757–October 10, 1773), killed by Indians near the Cumberland Gap; Israel (January 25, 1759–August 19, 1782), killed by Indians at the Battle of Blue Licks; Susannah (November 2, 1760–October 19, 1800); Jemima (October 4, 1762–August 30, 1834); Levina (March 23, 1766–April 6, 1802); Rebecca (May 26, 1768–July 14, 1805); Daniel Morgan (December 23, 1769–July 13, 1839); Jesse Bryan (May 23, 1773–1820); and William (born June 20, 1775; died in infancy). See Lilian Hays Oliver, *Some Boone Descendants and Kindred of the St. Charles District* (Rancho Cordova, CA: Dean Publications, 1984), 16–17.

72. This anecdote is found in DM 20C:84(52–54).

73. How much of this predictable soliloquy is from Boone is speculative. Most likely it is Peter Houston's embellishment of Filson's or Trumball's Boone biographies, or it may be F. W. Houston's paraphrase of Abbott. See Abbott, *Boone*, 281–83.

74. Peter Houston's panther-hunting anecdote is found in DM 20C:84(54–57).

75. Making tinder from cotton cloth is easy. Squares of 100 percent cotton cloth cut two or three inches wide are loosely piled in a small tin that has a couple of awl-size holes poked in the top and bottom, and the tin is set in a fire. In minutes smoke pours from the holes as the cotton chars and the impurities burn off. After twenty to thirty minutes, the can is taken off to cool. If all has gone well, the cloth will be blackened but strong enough that it will not crumble. Charred cloth, whether in a tinderbox or held in the hand, will easily catch a spark. See note 43; for more on frontier fire starting, see Warren "Hawk" Boughton, "Firemaking," in *The Book of Buckskinning II*, ed. William H. Scurlock (Texarkana, TX: Rebel Publishing Company, 1983), 149–72.

76. This romanticized tale is in DM 20C:84(57–64).

77. The narrative's reference to Nathan Boone in 1780 cannot be correct. Nathan was born March 2, 1781, at Boone's Station, Fayette County, Kentucky.

78. Whether or not Daniel Boone returned to Kentucky after 1799 to pay his debts is debatable. Firsthand reports abound of his twice visiting Kentucky in the early 1800s. Many such rumors are best seen as apocryphal, but some accounts are laced with convincing details, thus clouding the issue. In 1851, Nathan Boone told Draper that such reports were tall tales, that his father had vowed to never again set foot in Kentucky because of the unfair treatment he received in his land deals. Opinions on Boone's alleged return to Kentucky after 1799 are mixed among twentieth-century Boone biographers. In 1902, Reuben Gold Thwaites contended that Boone returned to Kentucky twice but does not say when. John Bakeless claims that Boone went back to Kentucky in 1810 and 1817, basing his writing on John James Audubon's reports. In 1976, Lawrence Elliott wrote that

Boone returned to Kentucky in 1810 and 1817, also most likely basing his words on Audubon's account. Dr. Michael A. Lofaro cites Audubon too, asserting that Boone returned in 1810 and 1817. In 1992, Dr. John Mack Faragher examined the issue and tends to side with Nathan Boone's declaration. See NB, 1851, DM 6S:231; John Mason Peck, *Life of Daniel Boone, the Pioneer of Kentucky* (Boston: Charles C. Little and James Brown, 1847), 192; Reuben Gold Thwaites, *Daniel Boone*, 2nd ed. (Williamstown, MA: Corner House Publishers, 1977), 222; Bakeless, *Boone*, 397–408; Michael A. Lofaro, *The Life and Adventures of Daniel Boone*, 2nd ed. (Lexington: University Press of Kentucky, 1986), 121–26; Lawrence Elliott, *The Long Hunter: A New Life of Daniel Boone* (New York: Reader's Digest Press, 1976), 197–99; JMF, 307–9.

79. Boone kept up his fall hunts during his Missouri years (1799–1820); he took his last hunt about 1817 when he was in his early eighties. Stephen Hempstead saw Boone, his son-in-law Flanders Callaway, and Boone's slave, Derry Coburn, landing a canoe near St. Louis. In Stephen Hempstead to LCD, March 6, 1863, DM 16C:78, Hempstead's glimpse of the old hunter's return from one of his last long hunts is vividly rendered:

I remember seeing them coming with hides over the cargo—a sure sign of her coming from the upper Missouri, and I went down to the landing to see who they were. The canoe was covered with bearskins. And she landed first the stern and the sternsman got out and then the bowsman rowed her around and they landed. This done to enable them to land and not disturb the cargo—the whole middle being full and covered. Mr. Flanders Callaway and the Negro rowed in front and Colonel Boone steered in the river. The face value of their furs and skins I cannot state, but it was considerable. I know also it was their constant practice to go by themselves or with two Negroes every winter to hunt—even long after all their friends were opposed to it—and Colonel Boone, I should suppose, then to be eighty years of age or upwards.

80. Eyewitness accounts of Boone's appearance and dress vary. As he is the best-known Long Hunter and has become the archetypal American frontiersman, a summary of these firsthand observations is useful. In 1774 Boone was seen near the Holston wearing a buckskin hunting shirt "dyed black"—most likely sewn from leather dyed in a broth of black walnut hulls. In 1780 John Redd saw Boone at Richmond while serving in the Virginia legislature as a representative of Kentucky: "He was dressed in real backwoods style, he had on a common jeans suit, with buckskin leggings beaded very neatly . . . manufactured by the Indians." In 1782 he was reportedly "dressed in a deerskin shirt and breeches." Christopher Mann told Lyman Draper that he once saw Boone "dressed in leather." On occasion, Boone wore a scarlet weskit with sterling buttons engraved with his name; the buttons were a gift from his nephew Daniel Bryan, who had made them in the fall of 1783. In 1791 Thomas Rodgers saw Boone at Maysville wearing a "linen hunting shirt and moccasins the color of leaves." Fielding Belt saw him at the Upper Blue Licks in 1799 dressed as "the poorest hunter" with his powderhorn, shot bag, rifle, and hunting shirt. Reverend James E. Welch described Boone in

1818 as "rather low of stature, broad shouldered, high cheek bones, very mild countenance [and] fair complexion." Reverend Timothy Flint, author of *Life and Exploits of Col. Dan'l Boone*, interviewed Boone in 1818 and observed that he had

> what phrenologists would have considered a model head—
> with a forehead peculiarly high, noble and bold—thin com-
> pressed lips—a mild clear blue eye—a large prominent chin,
> and a general expression of countenance in which fearlessness
> and courage sat enthroned. . . . Never was old age more green
> or gray hairs more graceful. His high, calm bold forehead
> seemed converted by his years into iron.

In an interview in 1851, Nathan Boone told Draper that his father stood five feet, eight inches and weighed 175 pounds but that near his death his weight dropped to 155 pounds. In 1868 Elijah Bryan observed that Boone "was one of the most powerful made men he ever knew—very straight, 5' 8"—heavy-made, thick thighs and very small ankles." William S. Bryan (1846–1940), coauthor of *Pioneer Families of Missouri*, related that Elijah Bryan said Boone was

> scarcely five feet eight inches . . . stout and heavy, and, until
> the last year or two of his life, inclined to corpulancy. His eyes
> were deep blue, and very brilliant, and were always on the
> alert. . . . His hair was gray, but had been originally light brown
> to flaxen, and was fine and soft.

For "dyed black," see Thwaites, *Boone*, 110; John Redd to LCD, c. 1848–49, DM 10NN:101; John Jones to LCD, 1868, DM 23S:207; Christopher Mann to LCD, October 15, 1883; Daniel Bryan to LCD, April 1844, DM 22C:14(14); Thomas Rodgers to LCD, 1863, DM 19S:168; Fielding Belt to LCD, 1866, DM 21S:204; James E. Welch, *Christian Repository*, Louisville, KY, March 1860, DM 16C:47–48; Timothy Flint, *Life and Exploits of Col. Dan'l Boone* (Philadelphia: H. M. Rulison, 1856), 249–50; NB to LCD, 1851, 6S:281; Elijah Bryan to LCD, c. 1868, DM 23S:243; William S. Bryan quoted in Oliver, *Boone Descendants*, 11–12.

81. Rebecca Boone died March 18, 1813, at age seventy-four. Daniel Boone died September 26, 1820, at age eighty-five. In 1845, amid much pomp and ceremony from local politicos and businesspeople, a delegation from Kentucky exhumed what were alleged to be the skeletons of Daniel and Rebecca Boone from the Boone-Bryan Cemetery on Tuque Creek, near St. Charles, Missouri, to take to Frankfort, Kentucky, for reinterment. But controversy shrouds the affair. Whether or not Kentuckians retrieved the right remains is yet an unsettled issue, and the true site of Boone's final resting place is the greatest of all Boone mysteries.

Bibliography

MANUSCRIPTS AND PAPERS

Draper Manuscripts. The State Historical Society of Wisconsin, Madison.

    Series B: Draper's "Life of Boone"

    Series C: Boone Papers

    Series S: Draper's Notes

    Series J: George Rogers Clark Papers

    Series NN: Pittsburgh and Northwest Virginia Papers

John Floyd Papers, May 1, 1776–March 28, 1783. Transcribed by Neal Owen Hammon.

F. W. Houston. "F. W. Houston's Letter to His Family Concerning Their Reunions," c. 1890.

———. "Lineage of Houston Family," July 4, 1895.

ARTICLES AND ANTHOLOGIES

Akers, Vincent. "The Low Dutch Company: A History of the Holland Dutch Settlements of the Kentucky Frontier." Reprinted from the Holland Society of history *de Halve Maen* 55, 2 (1980): 1-1-4, 21; 3 (1980): 12–15; 4 (1980): 9–13, 19–20; *de Halve Maen* 56, 1 (1981): 6–14.

Ardery, Mrs. William Breckenridge. *Historical Scrapbook: Bourbon County, Kentucky*. Paris, KY: Privately published, 1939.

Belue, Ted Franklin. "Battle of Blue Licks." In *The American Revolution, 1775–1783: An Encyclopedia*, vol. 1, edited by Dr. Richard L. Blanco, 133–36. New York: Garland Publishing, 1993.

———. "Black Fish." In *The Kentucky Encyclopedia*, edited by John E. Kleber, 84. Lexington: University Press of Kentucky, 1992.

———. "Blacks on the Western Frontier." In *The American Revolution,*

1775–1783: An Encyclopedia, vol. 1, edited by Dr. Richard L. Blanco, 128–29. New York: Garland Publishing, 1993.

———. "Crawford's Sandusky Expedition: May–June 1782." In *The American Revolution, 1775–1783: An Encyclopedia*, vol. 1, edited by Dr. Richard L. Blanco, 416–20. New York: Garland Publishing, 1993.

———. "Did Daniel Boone Kill Pompey, the Black Shawnee, at the 1778 Siege of Boonesborough?" *Filson Club History Quarterly* 67 (1993): 5–22.

———. "Indian-Influenced Woodsmen of the Cane." In *The Book of Buckskinning VII*, edited by William H. Scurlock, 42–77. Texarkana, TX: Scurlock Publishing Company, 1995.

———. "Siege of Bryan's Station Kentucky: August 15–17, 1782." In *The American Revolution, 1775–1783: An Encyclopedia*, vol. 1, edited by Dr. Richard L. Blanco, 189–91. New York: Garland Publishing, 1993.

———. "Terror in the Canelands: The Fate of Daniel Boone's Saltboilers." *Filson Club History Quarterly* 68 (1994): 3–34.

Boughton, Warren. "Firemaking." In *The Book of Buckskinning II*, edited by William H. Scurlock, 149–72. Texarkana, TX: Rebel Publishing Company, 1983.

Calloway, Colin C. "Neither White nor Red: White Renegades on the American Indian Frontier." *Western Historical Quarterly* 17, 1(1986): 43–66.

———. "Simon Girty: Interpreter and Intermediary." In *Being and Becoming Indian: Biographical Studies of North American Frontiers*, edited by James A. Clifton, 38–58. Prospect Heights, IL: Waveland Press, 1989.

Clark, Thomas D. "Salt: a Factor in the Settlement of Kentucky." *Filson Club History Quarterly* 12 (1938): 42–52.

Collins, Richard H. "The Siege of Bryan's Station." *Register of the Kentucky Historical Society* 36 (1938): 15–25.

Hammon, Neal Owen. "The Fincastle Surveyors at the Falls of the Ohio: 1774." *Filson Club History Quarterly* 47 (1973): 14–28.

———. "Fincastle Surveyors in the Bluegrass: 1774." *Register of the Kentucky Historical Society* 70 (1972): 277–94.

———. "Pioneers in Kentucky, 1773–1775." *Filson Club History Quarterly* 55 (1981): 2701–71.

———. "Pioneer Kentucky History: Separating the Facts from the Myths," n.p.

Hoffman, Philip. "Simon Girty." In *The American Revolution, 1775–1783: An Encyclopedia*, vol. 1, edited by Dr. Richard L. Blanco, 660–64. New York: Garland Publishing, 1993.

Hughes, Nicky. "Battle of Blue Licks." In *The Kentucky Encyclopedia*, edited by John Kleber, 92–93. Lexington: University Press of Kentucky, 1992.

Tapp, Hambleton. "Colonel John Floyd, Kentucky Pioneer," *Filson Club History Quarterly* 15 (1941): 1–24.

Welch, James E. *Christian Repository*. Louisville, KY, March 1860.

BOOKS

Abbott, John S. C. *Daniel Boone: Pioneer of Kentucky*. New York: Dodd and Mead, 1872.

Bakeless, John. *Daniel Boone: Master of the Wilderness*. 2nd ed. Lincoln, NE: Bison, 1989.

Belue, Ted Franklin. *The Long Hunt: Death of the Buffalo East of the Mississippi*. Mechanicsburg, PA: Stackpole Books, 1996.

Butterfield, Consul Wilshire. *History of the Girtys*. 2nd ed. Columbus, OH: Long's College Book Co., 1950.

Calloway, Colin G. *The American Revolution in Indian Country: Crisis and Diversity in Native American Communities*. New York: Cambridge University Press, 1995.

Draper, Lyman C. *King's Mountain and its Heroes*. 2nd ed. Baltimore: Baltimore Genealogical Publishing Company, 1969.

Elliott, Lawrence. *The Long Hunter: A New Life of Daniel Boone*. New York: Reader's Digest Press, 1976.

Faragher, John Mack. *Daniel Boone: The Life and Legend of an American Pioneer*. New York: Henry B. Holt, 1992.

Filson, John. *The Discovery, Settlement and Present State of Kentucke*. New York: Corinth Books, 1962. Originally published in 1784; many editions available.

Flint, Timothy. *Life and Exploits of Col. Dan'l Boone*. Philadelphia: H. M. Rulison, 1856. Originally published in 1833.

Hammon, Neal Owen. *Early Kentucky Land Records: 1773–80*. Filson Club Publication, 2nd ser., no. 5. Louisville, KY: Butler Book Company, 1992.

Hanna, Charles A. *The Wilderness Trail*. New York: Knickerbocker Press, 1911.

Hatley, Tom. *The Dividing Paths: Cherokees and South Carolinians through the Revolutionary Era*. New York: Oxford University Press, 1995.

Lester, William Stewart. *The Transylvania Company*. Spencer, IN: Samuel R. Guard and Company, 1939.

Lofaro, Michael A. *The Life and Adventures of Daniel Boone*. 2nd ed. Lexington: University Press of Kentucky, 1986.

O'Malley, Nancy. *Stockading Up: A Study of Pioneer Stations in the Inner Bluegrass Region of Kentucky*. Archaeological Report 127. Frankfort: Kentucky Heritage Council, 1987.

Oliver, Lilian Hays. *Some Boone Descendants and Kindred of the St. Charles District*. Rancho Cordova, CA: Dean Publications, 1984.

Peck, John Mason. *Life of Daniel Boone, the Pioneer of Kentucky*. Boston: Charles C. Little and James Brown, 1847.

Spraker, Hazel Atterbury. *The Boone Family*. Baltimore: Genealogical Publishing Company, 1974.

Thwaites, Reuben Gold. *Daniel Boone*. 2nd ed. Williamstown, MA: Corner House Publishers, 1977.

Turner, Frederick Jackson. *The Frontier in American History*. 3rd ed. Malabar, FL: Robert E. Krieger Press, 1985.

Young, Charles Raymond, ed. *Westward into Kentucky: The Memoirs of Daniel Trabue*. Lexington: University Press of Kentucky, 1981.

Suggested Reading

DANIEL BOONE

John Bakeless, *Daniel Boone: Master of the Wilderness*, 3rd ed. (Lincoln, NE: Bison, 1989).

Lawrence Elliott, *The Long Hunter: A New Life of Daniel Boone* (New York: Reader's Digest Press, 1976).

John Mack Faragher, *The Life and Legend of an American Pioneer* (New York: Henry B. Holt, 1992).

John Filson, *The Discovery, Settlement and Present State of Kentucke* (Wilmington, DE: James Adams, 1784). Many modern editions are available.

Michael A. Lofaro, *The Life and Adventures of Daniel Boone* (Lexington, KY: University Press of Kentucky, 1978).

Elizabeth A. Moize, "Daniel Boone: First Hero of the Frontier," *National Geographic*, 186 (1985), 812–41.

Richard Slotkin, *Regeneration Through Violence: The Mythology of the American Frontier, 1600–1860*, 2nd ed. (New York: HarperPerennial, 1996).

J. Gray Sweeney, *The Columbus of the Woods: Daniel Boone and the Typology of Manifest Destiny*, (St. Louis: Washington University Gallery of Art, 1992).

BOONE GENEALOGY

Lilian Hays Oliver, *Some Boone Descendants and Kindred of the St. Charles District* (Rancho Cordova, CA: Dean Publications, 1984).

Hazel Atterbury Spraker, *The Boone Family*, 2nd ed. (Baltimore: Genealogical Publishing Company, 1974).

KENTUCKY FRONTIER LIFE

Harriette Simpson Arnow, *Seedtime on the Cumberland*, 2nd ed. (Lexington, KY: University Press of Kentucky, 1983).

Stephen Aron, *How the West Was Lost: The Transformation of Kentucky from Daniel Boone to Henry Clay* (Baltimore: Johns Hopkins University Press, 1996).

John Bradford, *The Voice of the Frontier: John Bradford's Notes on Kentucky*, edited by Thomas D. Clark (Lexington, KY: University Press of Kentucky, 1993).

Thomas D. Clark, *A History of Kentucky* (Lexington, KY: John Bradford Press, 1960).

William Stewart Lester, *The Transylvania Colony* (Spencer, IN: Samuel R. Guard and Company, 1935).

Allan W. Eckert, *The Frontiersman: A Narrative* (Boston: Little, Brown and Company, 1967).

Arthur K. Moore, *The Frontier Mind*, 2nd ed. (New York: McGraw-Hill, 1963).

George W. Ranck, *Boonesborough* (Louisville, KY: John P. Morton and Company, 1901).

Otis K. Rice, *Frontier Kentucky* (Lexington, KY: University Press of Kentucky, 1978).

Charles Gano Talbert, *Benjamin Logan: Kentucky Frontiersman* (Lexington, KY: University Press of Kentucky, 1962).

Daniel Trabue, *Westward into Kentucky: The Memoirs of Daniel Trabue*, edited by Chester Raymond Young (Lexington, KY: University Press of Kentucky, 1981).

KENTUCKY INDIAN WARS

Consul Wilshire Butterfield, *History of the Girtys* (Columbus, OH: Robert Clarke and Company, 1950).

Richard H. Collins, "The Siege of Bryan's Station," *Register of the Kentucky State Historical Society*, 36 (1938), 15–25.

Gregory Evans Dowd, *A Spirited Resistance: The North American Indian Struggle for Unity, 1745–1815* (Baltimore: Johns Hopkins University Press, 1993).

Randolph C. Downes, *Council Fires on the Upper Ohio: A Narrative of Indian Affairs in the Upper Ohio Valley until 1795*, 3rd ed. (Pittsburgh: University of Pittsburgh Press, 1977).

Allan W. Eckert, *That Dark and Bloody River* (New York: Bantam Books, 1995).

Michael N. McConnell, *A Country Between: The Upper Ohio Valley and Its People, 1724-1774* (Lincoln, NE: University of Nebraska Press).

George W. Ranck, *The Story of Bryan's Station* (Louisville, KY: John P. Morton and Company, 1896).

O. M. Spencer, *The Indian Captivity of O. M. Spencer*, 2nd ed. (New York: Dover Publications, Inc., 1995).

Samuel M. Wilson, *Battle of the Blue Licks* (Lexington, KY: privately published, 1927).

Bennett H. Young, *History of the Battle of Blue Licks* (Louisville, KY: John P. Morton and Company, 1897).

Index